P9-BIY-596

For The Facing Of This Hour

A CALL TO ACTION

by
J. Alfred Smith, Sr.

Progressive Baptist Publishing House
850 North Grove Ave.
Elgin, IL 60120

Contents

FOR THE FACING OF THIS HOUR

Progressive Baptist Publishing House, Elgin, IL 60120

Printed in the United States of America
Library of Congress Catalog Number: 81-74074
ISBN: 0-89191-267-3

Preface

THESE MESSAGES WERE GIVEN in lectures at Baylor University, Ouachita University, University of the Redlands, Southwestern Baptist Theological Seminary, the University of California Medical School in San Francisco, the Baptist World Alliance in Toronto, Canada, and the annual meeting of the Progressive National Baptist Convention.

I am deeply grateful to Dr. Boynkin Sanders, Professor of New Testament at Andover Newton Theological School for reading the manuscript and offering helpful suggestions and criticisms. James W. English, of David C. Cook Publishing Company, helped to improve this manuscript and gave me needed encouragement. President L. Doward McBain and Dean Lee Hine granted me sabbatical time along with the American Baptist Seminary of the West, which gave me faculty support. Dean Lee Hine gave major assistance in this project.

To these friends I am also grateful: The typing assistance of Miss Billie Poole and Mrs. Joanne Pike, the proofreading of Anthony and Faye Smith, my son and daughter-in-law, the advice and love of my wife, as well as the understanding of the Allen Temple membership made it possible for me to write in an environment of peace and acceptance.

It is with reservation and caution that I put my thoughts into print, inasmuch as no human word is ultimate, and moreover, I am sure this manuscript is not even the penultimate. Nevertheless, I am confident that God will use my efforts to inspire us to become courageously participants with Jesus, the living lord of history, in creating on the stage of history a useable future.

The purpose of this book is to challenge us to summon the future with heroic action in the present, and to remind us of our theological basis for living with courage for today and hope for tomorrow.

The author did not have time to adequately address the dangers of a nuclear confrontation, and regrets this omission.

J. Alfred Smith, Sr.
Oakland, California
August 1981

To Jo Anna, my wife of thirty years, and to our inquisitive grandchildren as well as to all of my students at Allen Temple in Oakland, American Baptist Seminary of the West in Berkeley, and Golden Gate Baptist Theological Seminary in Mill Valley.

For the Facing of This Hour: A Call to Action

WILLIAM BUTLER YEATS has described this hour to perfection:

> Things fall apart; the center cannot hold,
> Mere anarchy is loosed upon the world . . .
> The best lack all conviction, while the worst
> Are full of passionate intensity.
>   (The Second Coming)

The erosion of time-tested traditions, the withering of moral values, the disdain for the church, and the despair with which the uncharted course of world history is rapidly moving are characteristics of this hour. Mechanization continues to speed the process of depersonalization. Technology has not always blessed society; it has on occasion cursed humanity with totalitarian manipulation; that is to say, dictators and persons of oppressive mentality have used modern knowledge in destructive ways.

Rabbi Robert Gordis in his work, *Leave a Little to God,* has spoken of desensitization, which makes people impervious to the promptings of conscience or apathetic toward the sufferings of others. Hence he says: "We have no poor, only the lower income brackets. Two-thirds of the world's children and millions in the United States are not perpetually hungry; they are merely suffering from malnutrition."[1] Our own experiences undergird the Gordis testimony.

FOR THE FACING OF THIS HOUR

Our own testimony says that when crime exists one block from our church sanctuaries, when injustice raises its demonic head in our communities, too often we refuse to get involved in the solution process. We behave as if those who are offended are not like us. We preach the gospel of a Banfield, who in his unheavenly city blames the victim for all of the problems of the inner city. Perhaps Peter Berger is accurate in describing "the noise of our solemn assemblies." Our religion often fails to bring harmony to the dissonance of secular culture.

If Oliver Goldsmith were alive today, he might be tempted to lament:

Ill fares the land, to hastening ills a prey,
Where wealth accumulates, and men decay.

With Dr. Paul Tillich, we can concur that our very foundations are shaking. Have we exhausted all of our possibilities? Have we not passed through three historical cycles? First humankind was nothing and God was everything. Then God was nothing and humankind was everything. Now God is nothing and humankind is nothing.

Behind the alternating bluster and blandness of our enemies, the ineptness and ignorance of our own leadership, behind the wealth of science and the spiritual poverty of persons, we are hearing voices of doom that cry, "Nothing art thou and unto nothing shalt thou return!" But louder than the noise of jet planes roaring over our heads, and more powerful than the blast of atomic explosions, those of us who leave the outer world for the inward journey into the citadel of the human spirit cannot help but hear that paradoxical voice that spoke with mysterious stillness to Moses, Elijah, the prophets, and Jesus. That voice gives us courage for the facing of this hour. Lo' tohu bera' ah lashevet yetzarah, which means, "God created the world not for chaos, but for human habitation." If there is chaos in the world today, it is the tohu vabhohu, the chaos before creation, the pain before birth, the confusion preceding a new day. I believe that our unfinished society affords the church an opportunity to become God's

copartner in the work of creation. This deep, abiding conviction enables me to face this hour with courage and hope. No
matter how long and agonizing our night may be, the dawn
will surely come if we remain awake, alert, and active in
mission for Him who does all things well.

Dr. Major Jones, in his work *Christian Ethics for Black Theology*, talks about courage and hope. He says:

> That utopian hope has always been a transforming ele-
> ment in the black religious experience. It has always
> rejected an insipid faith and an insensitive ethic by
> holding faith and ethics together in a life of courage in
> suffering and hope, and hope in courage and suffering.
> Existentially, all men of utopian hope have transformed
> history; they have not been transformed by history . . .
> The Birmingham jail was surely equal to Attica, but
> because his hope (Dr. Martin Luther King, Jr.) was uto-
> pian, the Birmingham jail became the occasion for one
> of the greatest letters of modern times. For the blacks at
> Attica, it was an occasion of death and ultimate an-
> nihilation. Blacks at Attica had lost hope. Utopian hope
> is transforming for the simple reason that it makes it
> possible for the person of hope to reject injustice without
> ceasing to acclaim the nature of man and the beauty of
> this world.[2]

I believe that those of us who are God's earthen vessels
must carry the content of a utopian hope in order to share it
with persons who have been bruised by brutality and
wounded by the outrageous arrows of injustice. I believe that
the search for a useable future and the discovery of credibility
for our hope will be found by non-Christians when heralds of
hope take powerful prophetic positions against the evils hid-
den in the personal, social, and institutional dimensions of
society. In the face of approaching disaster, eighth-century
prophets like Isaiah spoke of the remnant that would survive.
This remnant was God's living sign for supreme hope. Abraham J. Heschel, in his work *The Prophets*, exclaimed that

"beyond the hope that a remnant would return was the ultimate hope that the whole world would be transformed."

Even God's anger has sorrow in it. Compassion is present in God's criticism. Hope is present in chastisement and judgment. God's anger must not conceal His redeeming love.

> Behold, God is my salvation; I will trust, and not be afraid: for the Lord JEHOVAH is my strength and my song; he also is become my salvation (Isaiah 12:2).

The Word of God speaks to this hour. When you and I decipher God's Word for this hour, we must understand that the Word of God never comes to an end. No word is God's final Word. He is always ready to bring a change in His judgment if there is a change in man's conduct. This hour can be faced with the assurance that the God who hurts also heals. Sometimes He hurts in order to heal and to meet our needs.

The needs of this hour, the plight and blight that infect the mental, moral, and spiritual life of the nation demand that we remember Leon W. Watts' philosophy that "either we move forward into . . . dazzling newness with fear and trembling, or we retreat to positions which will be at least temporarily more familiar and more comfortable."

Shall we retreat when in our ghettos people live in the most dilapidated and unhealthful sections of our cities? Shall we retreat while our election districts are so gerrymandered that the white poor and racial minorities find it impossible to secure elected officials who represent their interests? Shall we seek comfort when the government has evaded compliance with laws that provide wholesome job opportunities for all? Shall we retreat when school districts controlled by racists provide our youth with segregated, inferior education? Shall we move to the rear while the United States has denied minority groups personhood by refusing to teach the heritage and the magnificent contributions to the life, wealth, and growth of this nation which have been made by people of color? Shall we passively move to the other side of our streets with the noninvolved while Black Muslims do economic development and Black Panthers in Oakland feed hungry children? How shall we face this hour? Shall we be at ease in Zion when our third-world brothers and sisters die daily at the hands of self-righteous sinners whose dollar power gives false justification to a "white man's burden ideology"?

Shall we move the wheel of progress backward to the time of the desacralization of nature so as to open the door for the birth of our ecological sins of polluting and poisoning the holy earth? Have we not moved to the place where in our visceral-level thinking the earth is no longer the Lord's and the universe no longer testifies of His architectural skill?

How shall we face this hour? Will we meet this challenge with courageous creativity and daring prophetic faith? Will we face the looming, leering negatives of this hour with the *Yes* of a resurrection faith that helps us begin again as members of the new creation in Christ? Will we? It is possible! Poet Wallace Stevens reminds us that the dry bones of our spiritual skeleton can live again. He says: "Under every *No* lay a passion for *Yes* that had never been broken."

What I mean is summed up in the words of Louis Untermeyer in his poem, "Prayer":

God, though this life is but a wraith,
Although we know not what we use,
Although we grope with little faith,
Give me the heart to fight—and lose.

Ever insurgent let me be,
Make me more daring than devout;
From sleek contentment keep me free,
And fill me with a buoyant doubt.

Open my eyes to vision girt
With beauty, and with wonder lit
But let me always see the dirt,
And all that spawn and die in it.

Open my ears to music; let
Me thrill with Spring's first flutes and drums

FOR THE FACING OF THIS HOUR

But never let me dare forget
The bitter ballads of the slums.

From compromise and things half done,
Keep me with stern and stubborn pride;
And when at last the fight is won,
God, keep me still unsatisfied.

An Address by Pastor J. Alfred Smith
For The Ministers and Missionaries Benefit Board Luncheon
Shiloh Baptist Church—Baltimore, Maryland
March 21, 1975
and to Baylor University, Waco, Texas in a lectureship in 1977

FOOTNOTES:

[1]Robert Gordis, *Leave a Little to God*, Bloch Publishing Co., New York, 1974, p. 5.

[2]Dr. Major Jones, *Christian Ethics for Black Theology*, Abingdon Press, Nashville, TN., 1974, p. 197.

[3]Louis Untermeyer, Harcourt, Brace and World, Inc., N.Y., 1914D1942.

Preparation for Sharing
and
Bearing the Good News

A placard on a city bus in Minneapolis read: "In this day every American needs to find God—Go to church Sunday." But someone had written in pencil at the bottom, "I went and He was not there." This story is indicative of the cynical manner in which many persons view the church.

Sterling A. Brown deals with their disillusionment in teaching: "God may be the owner, but He's rich and forgetful and faraway." Some argue that God is an absentee landlord. "Conspirators of darkness and celebrants of the grotesque" question the existence of God. Dr. Cecil Cone, President of Edward Waters College in Jacksonville, Florida, helps us to see that many persons are outside of the Christian family because they do not understand how evil can be present where a loving God holds the whole world in His hand. This study is called theodicy or the justice of God. The theological dilemma is that either God is not all-powerful and thus unable to do anything about the evil in the world, or that He is all-powerful and unjust because He will not do anything about it.

The late Dr. Edgar Sheffield Brightman of Boston University postulated a thesis that God is not omnipotent but is a self-limited God. Brightman argued that this God of self-limitations allows persons to construct evil designs with the

15

freedom of human choice. Brightman also taught the dogma of a suffering, self-limited God who cares for persons and who struggles with persons against evil.

Other thinkers see evil as an illusion. Some others see evil as the absence of good. Still others argue an oriental yin and yang thesis, that the nature of reality is a mixture of good and evil. The disciples of deism depict divinity as the master designer or watchmaker who winds up the world like a clock and then sits back to watch the world run itself down. Still others see reality from an atheistic posture of a self-existing, ever-expanding universe.

The modern market place of ideas is securing from the black community more and more customers for its sub-Christian philosophies. Many of these young people come from Christian backgrounds, but after sitting down at the philosophical banquet table to eat an atheistic meal prepared for them by secular scholars, they soon forget the religious roots of their parents, who are subsidizing their tuition with money earned by prayers, pain, and personal sacrifice. All of these persons challenge us to evangelize this secular world.

The evangelizing of this modern world is not an easy task. Christians cannot win thinking and nonthinking people to Jesus Christ by simply sharing their conversion experience. Nor can Christians win people to Jesus Christ with sincerity and good intentions. Evangelism needs courageous, committed, consecrated persons who know both Jesus of history, and the Christ of experience, as well as to know how to discuss intelligently the tenets of the faith with unbelievers.

With the growth of cults in the black community, the multiplication of Jehovah's Witnesses, and the infatuation of so-called sophisticates with Science of the Mind groups, together with the heavy emphasis upon Transcendental Meditation, it is late in the afternoon, but not too late for churches to take their members out of a spiritual kindergarten in order to train them to be tough in mind and tender in heart as bearers and sharers of the good news.

Special effort should be made to evangelize not only individuals, but also families. Trained foot soldiers in the infantry of evangelism should know techniques and methods as well as Biblical and theological principles for sharing the good news. I argue for special effort in reaching families with the Gospel, because a people without a strong family structure becomes a people without a future. Dr. Obie Wright, Sr., Assistant Professor of Theology at School of Religion, Howard University, Washington, D.C. said that without a vision of liberation in Christ, "The soul of a man, of a woman rots and pollutes the creative stream surrounding its gates." Pollution must be present when 63 percent of black youth are unemployed, out of school and possessors of a jail record. About 35 percent of black youth are lost on hard drugs.

These telling facts have implications for our preparation for sharing and bearing the good news. Good evangelistic preparation requires the skills for saving a young woman from the pitiful profession of prostitution. But good evangelistic preparation must join hands with Christian social concerns to upgrade the public schools, and provide meaningful employment for people so that prostitution will not be an easy attraction for unemployed young women.

Preparation for telling the good news means that God is concerned about the moral and spiritual health of the environment in which new Christians are to be nurtured. Just as beautiful flowers need for their environment good, rich, black soil, so do Christian persons become Christlike when the soil of good environment is free from the weeds of exploitation, greed, sensuality, and immorality.

Immoral structures of religion, government, politics, and business, where moral persons work, need redemption from their decadence. An immoral institution can crush and cripple a moral person who works for that institution. The cry for righteousness must be personal and social. The announcement of God's kingdom must be both to the individual and the group. Christ must be not only in the soul of the business person, but also in the soul of the business. Prepared bearers and sharers of the Gospel must know how to touch the person and the social structures of society with the call and claims of the Gospel.

FOR THE FACING OF THIS HOUR

What is the Gospel? Why is the Gospel called good news? Is the good news more than the individual's love of Jesus? Is good news simply the telling of a Bible story? Is the good news shallow, pious, religious sentimentality?

I answer very simply that the Gospel is a love story of the one and only holy God, who through His Son, Jesus Christ, expressed His total, unqualified acceptance of us. This definition tells us about God, God's Son, and ourselves. An amplification of the definition states that God's Word to us is expressed in the life, death, and resurrection of Jesus Christ. I realize that my definition is conservative and far too limited for the liberal theologians, and perhaps not narrow enough for theological fundamentalism. However, my posture is that the Old Testament is Jesus Christ concealed and the New Testament is Jesus Christ revealed.

I argue that God's Word addresses us in twofold form; stereophonically rather than monophonically. By this I mean that when God speaks, you and I hear sterephonically the God of wrath and the God of mercy. When God speaks, we hear His condemnation of our sins, and His offer of forgiveness.

The reformers, such as Luther, believed that God's law must be proclaimed with all its power to convict persons of sin. God's grace must be spoken with all its potency so that the sinner would have the message of God's acceptance of the unacceptable. Heinrich Ott in explaining the Heidelberg Catechism touches upon three important points:

1. Man's "sin and wretchedness"
2. the "redemption" wrought on our behalf by God through Christ, and
3. the obligations of gratitude which God's redeeming act lays upon us.

These three points are basic for sharing and bearing the Gospel.

1. Man's lostness in sin before God;
2. The redemptive work of Jesus as our Lord and Saviour, and
3. Our grateful obedience to God's Word.

Preparation for sharing and bearing the good news requires that you and I stop long enough to prepare ourselves for proclaiming God's message to a lost world. Preparation is serious business and it should be carefully done. Preparation understands that the Gospel is first of all bad news and secondly, good news. In theological jargon this is called law and the Gospel. Martin Luther saw law as "the hammer of judgment" and Paul Tillich saw law as "the mirror of existence." The law is a "large and powerful hammer" with which God smashes our pretentions and brings us to our knees. Thus, the law can be a most useful servant bringing us to Christ as a mirror, the law helps us to see ourselves. The law always accuses. It helps us to enter into the court of God's morality with the plea of guilty.

The Gospel releases us from guilt and from the bondage of the law. The Gospel declares that sinners are righteous in Christ. The Gospel invites us to accept Christ's invitation: "Come unto me, all ye that labour and are heavy laden, and I will give you rest" (Matthew 11:28).

It is so easy for us to interpret Jesus' offer to rest as meaning to relax in the rocking chair of lazy religion. The invitation of Jesus calls us to the ministry of cross bearing. Dr. Joseph A. Johnson, Presiding Bishop of the Fourth Episcopal District, has said: "The cross is a natural symbol of crossroads, and therefore, of decision, crisis, choice, of being crossed, of frustration, adversity, fate, and finally, to the artistic eye, a cross is a figure of a man."

You may ask: What is God doing while evil rages and justice sleeps? You may ask: Where is God, inasmuch as demons of destruction are now tasting the bread of success? I ask you to take another look at a hill called Calvary. At that place of a skull, the sufferings of God for us reached a climax. Prior to Calvary, He was denied shelter, rejected by His kinsmen, ridiculed in public. He was knocked down and walked on as a door mat. He was betrayed by friends, oppressed by the power structure. But at Calvary, He wore a crown of thorns. At Calvary His hands and feet were nailed to the cross. At Calvary blood and water trickled down in a slow

19

stream that became a fountain filled with blood drawn from Emmanuel's veins. At Calvary the great shepherd of the sheep became the bleeding lamb. At Calvary a lifted-up Saviour reaches down and lifts me up to a harmonious relationship with the everlasting Father.

Though I do not have all the answers to the mysteries of life and death, though Jesus is more than my mind can define, I must be a herald prepared to announce the good news. I must be a witness prepared to testify of His grace.

I must be prepared to speak to the theodicy question of suffering in general and the long years of disproportionate black suffering that has troubled thinking blacks to question God's love and justice. This unbelief was called sin by Paul Tillich. It led to hubris which Tillich called the self-evaluation of man into the arena of the divine. Hubris, which is the self-evaluation of man, may also become the self-evaluation of a group. When a group, nation, or institution confuses positive and healthy self-affirmation with destructive self-elevation, demonic or sinful behavior has taken place. In a racist world where some groups have pushed destructive self-elevation and determined self-advantage over other groups, the oppressed can easily wonder where good news can be found. What good news can you give an unemployed father denied opportunities because of race? What hope can you give the young mother whose child is doing poorly in school because inferior educational opportunities killed the child's mind at an early age? What good news is there for prisoners wasting away in prisons as forgotten men?

I answer your questions with good news—Jesus, Himself came as good news. He was Emmanuel, which means "God is with us." So I say God is with us in pursuit of liberation. Our Gospel is about a rugged and robust Jesus who for our sakes trod the winepress of suffering alone.

I hear your voices, critics! You say, let God become a Jew, a poor black Jew. Let Him be born in one of the smaller exploited countries of the world ruled by the iron hand of some great foreign power. Let God experience persecution,

20

poverty, discrimination, prejudice and oppression. Let God be possessed with a great idea about the kind of world in which men ought to live and let Him teach His ideas to the people of His own group. Let God be betrayed by those who profess to love Him and be forsaken by His closest friends when He is caught in the iron vise of the governmental rulers of His day. Let God be condemned unjustly and the verdict of guilty be pronounced upon Him. Let a cross be placed on His back and let Him be whipped up some hill and suffer the most excruciating death that man can devise—crucifixion. Let God be nailed to that cross and hang between heaven and earth, deserted, forsaken, and alone. Let Him die there alone, alone, alone.

Well, critics this is what took place on Calvary. But you argue that this was bad news. I answer no, it was not bad news.

God entered my arena and became just like me; teaching me at Calvary, not only how sinful I can be in crucifying good, but also how good I can become in Christ as I, like Him, stand tiptoe on the peak of morality and pray genuinely for my enemies: Father! Forgive them. *Is not this good news?*

God at Calvary says that I, the unacceptable, have become acceptable. *Isn't that good news?* God at Calvary tells us to wait until Easter for victory. Isn't the resurrection good news? Isn't the final coming of Jesus good news? Let us prepare to share and bear the good news of Jesus Christ by:

1. becoming courageous, committed, consecrated persons who know both Jesus of history and the Christ of experience; by
2. becoming skilled in knowing how to explain the meaning of the good news story in the modern market place of ideas where cults, atheism, and agnosticism compete for the control of the minds and hearts of people; and
3. by action that will move the church into public places to penetrate secular culture with the Gospel and its meaning for personal and social salvation.

21

FOR THE FACING OF THIS HOUR

The Conclusion

There is joy in sharing and bearing good news. In spite of our failures and our disloyalties to truth, there is the good news of God's forgiveness for our sins. There is God's offer of reconciliation for our alienation. There is the promise of the kingdoms of this world becoming the kingdom of His Lord, and our Christ! There is the promise of a new Jerusalem to replace this sinful Babylon. Joyfully let us go everywhere with this message. Joyfully, though we may not have silver and gold, we can proceed with Jesus' word. Man cannot live by bread *alone*. God has entrusted us with this message. Let us prepare our hearts and minds to tell it. Let us go into the avenues, the barrios, the boulevards, the corners of crowded streets, the dives of the demonic with an eagerness to tell the story. Let us go to the ghettos, even to Sugar Hill. Go tell it!

"Although the fig tree shall not blossom, neither shall fruit be on the vines; the labour of the olive shall fail, and the fields shall yield no meat, the flock shall be cut off from the fold, and there shall be no herd in the stalls: Yet I will rejoice in the Lord, I will joy in the God of my salvation" (Heb. 3:17-18).

Redigging the Wells
of Our Fathers
(Genesis 26:17-25)

In Isaac's day, wells were a part of living as much as light was a part of day. Clog up the wells with debris and death would come. Without well water the hot and tired traveler, sick and sore from summer's blistering heat, would soon die in his tracks. A dried-up well meant no food for cooking or cleansing. An empty well meant no water for the cattle of the field or the food of the farm. A failure of the well to produce water meant that the greenery of the forest and the foliage of flowers would soon turn to a dry and dusty place of sand dunes and death. Water was life and to have life was to have water.

Men fought to kill over the best watering holes. Ranches and farmers, cattlemen and tillers of the soil, rich and poor fought each other for the land which had rivers and lakes. If none existed, then they would seek out that land which had underground springs. On that land, wells would be dug. The Bible has much to say about wells. It refers to Jacob's well or to Abraham's well. Our text mentions Isaac who dug new wells, but was also forced to redig the wells of his father, Abraham.

My message must make clear the point that you and I are like Isaac as it relates to wells. We must dig new wells that will give life to our children. We must also redig the wells our fathers dug for us.

FOR THE FACING OF THIS HOUR

The text words tell us that Abraham's father dug wells and named them for him. Abraham dug wells for his son, Isaac, and he gave the wells the same names used by his father. But Philistines came on the scene as enemies and stopped up the wells so that Isaac could not use them.

Our fathers have dug wells of survival for us, but Philistines are at work filling up those wells.

Some of us who still have water to drink are so blind that we cannot see our wells drying up. Some say to me there are no Philistines, and no wells are being filled in. We have as much water as we ever had. If people do not have water, it is because they are lazy; we have plenty of water. I answer with the serious and sober voice of sanity that there are Philistines hurting us, and I can call their names.

1. Mr. Bakke is a Philistine trying to dry up the wells of equal educational opportunity for all. Schools like Harvard and Yale were built for the aristocrats, and not us. Special preferences have always been the blessings of aristocrats.

2. Jarvis and Gann are Philistines, where Proposition 13 will harm renters, civil service persons, government workers, the minorities, the aged, and the last hired, more than it will save money for all concerned. An increase in sale taxes, and city and state taxes, will hurt persons on fixed incomes far more than those who are well off. Jarvis and Gann are closing up the wells of economic justice. Cities where we live will hurt far more than suburbia.

3. The revival of the Ku Klux Klan in America, the growth of the American Nazi Party, the increase of racial incidents experienced by blacks in the military who are overseas in places like Germany, or, here at military bases, the increase of segregated schools in our northern cities, and the continual increases of cities that are becoming all black, indicate to me that fact that racism is filling up the wells of integration dug by our fathers. Marcus Garvey, Malcolm X, Martin Luther King, Jr., W. E. B. DuBois, and Medgar Evers, were among those fa-

thers whose wells are being filled in so that you and I
cannot drink from them. American business interests are
also preventing new wells of liberation from being dug
in South Africa.

What are we to do? Shall we sit at ease in Zion? Shall we
delude ourselves into believing that trouble will evaporate
into thin air? Shall we hide our heads in the sands of religios-
ity, expecting God to do for us what we can do for ourselves?

We can help ourselves. We can unify our divided selves. We
can trust each other. We can pray and pull together. We can
sing and serve together. We can work and work together. We
can clean up our communities of drugs, decay, and destruction. We can redig the wells of our fathers. From redug wells
we can drink the purifying waters of decency, and dignity.
From wells that we redug, just as Isaac redug the wells of his
father Abraham, we can drink the waters of purity, pride,
freedom, and respect.

These are difficult days. Troubles never end. When we
solve one problem, another comes. When we sit down to rest
from one struggle, a new one challenges us. When we put out
one fire, a new one starts. When we defeat one enemy, a new
one confronts us. The rains that fell yesterday do not quench
today's thirst. Well-diggers leave us wells, and change this
earthly existence for a timeless one. We honor them in death;
call them heroes in our history, and sit back to refresh ourselves from the wells they left us. But Philistines have put
trash in the wells, while we were sleeping. What must we do?
We are now tired and tormented. We are sad, sorrowful, and
sick, and our thirst is unsatisfied. What must we do? We
thought that things were getting better. We thought that each
generation was seeing progress, but instead we see an evil
world much wiser and more wicked than the evil world of
yesterday! What must we do? How can we cope? How did our
fathers cope?

I will tell you how they coped. I will tell you what we must
do! As did our fathers, we need living water! Jesus gave them
living water. It was not from the well. Living water helped to
unify them; it kept them walking, talking, and praying to-

gether all along this tedious journey. Together, they looked to the Lord. Together, they fought Philistines, redug old wells for themselves, and new wells for us, their children. I have tasted that water. Have you tasted it?

Christian friends, let us dig new wells for our children, and let us redig the wells of our fathers.

The Christian Mother
and the Church Covenant
(Matthew 1:23)

When Mark Antony stood to eulogize Julius Caesar, he said: "Friends, Romans, countrymen, lend me your ears; I come to bury Caesar, not to praise him." My claim to you is: I have come today not to eulogize motherhood with sentimental words. I have come to challenge women to recognize that in God's eyes the high honor of motherhood is reached by climbing the high hill of heavy responsibilities. Does not the church covenant say: To religiously educate our children. Modern mothers, in the name of freedom, have ceased to religiously educate our children, as seriously and strictly as many of yesterday's mothers.

Non-Christian mothers, to some extent, are a part of the negative forces of women's liberation movements. Some of these women are "wolves in sheep's clothing." Under the disguise of liberation, they advocate abortions, even when they are not for medical reasons. Nonmedical reasons for abortions disregard the sacredness of the new life that the mothers of our permissive society carry in their bodies. A minority of non-Christian leaders of women's liberation are using their own God-given freedom to suit themselves when they adopt a lesbian lifestyle. However it is immoral to use women's liberation as a cover or front for promoting lesbianism. Women who have been beaten or violently treated by mentally sick and emotionally insecure men, are an easy prey for lesbians who practice their trade under the banner of freedom and equality for women. Husbands who are cruel to their wives and unmarried men who treat women disgracefully must bear their share of blame for more and more women turning to lesbianism. Irresponsible motherhood may overpopulate the world, but lesbianism is the poorest of the known methods of planned parenthood.

Let us look seriously at our text. Matthew 1:23 says: "Behold, a virgin shall be with child." It did not say a husband and wife, or a woman and man shall copulate, egg and sperm meeting, and a child shall be born. The doctrine of Mary as a virgin is God's greatest compliment to womanhood. Mary is the mother of Jesus, our Saviour. God lets us have a divine Saviour only with the help of Mary, the woman. Men may have been great prophets like Isaiah, Jeremiah and Ezekiel, and famous writers like Matthew, Mark, Luke, and noted orators like Peter and Paul, but only Mary, the woman, could copulate with God Himself for the birth, and rearing of Jesus our Lord. God is not a male chauvinist. God said to women: You are special. Too many women are saying we don't want to be special. We want to deny our special status by coming down from the high peak of morality. In the valley of immorality we can compete with men for championship in the dirty sports of cursing, coarseness, and crassness. We can chase men, before they can chase us, making every day Sadie Hawkins Day, and every year leap year.

Girls, and teenagers who aspire to be mothers, be prepared for motherhood before you become a mother. Prepare yourself spiritually, mentally, morally and physically. Don't run off from home and marry (a male), just to leave home. Be prepared to offer your unborn children more than a physical body. But you should offer at least a good physical body. If you abuse your mind and body with drugs, joints, alcohol, and needles as well as promiscuity, you will bring into the world deformed and retarded children. Be prepared to teach morals, self-respect, respect for others, respect for the property of others, and above all, respect for God.

Be prepared to supervise the study habits of your children. Don't wait until open house at the schools. Visit the schools of your children. Support the teachers of your children. Be qualified when you marry to give your husband thoughtful, supportive, shared interest in his daily work. He needs a trained woman with skills. He needs push and prayers when those outside the home pressure him with words of defeat and disgust. He needs you by his side in success and failure. No matter how educated and independent you become, please remember to stroke your man's fragile ego with Eve's touch of feminity, so that he will feel needed, wanted, and loved by you.

If you do all that I am asking you to do, and your man is unable to respond with love to this kind of treatment, he is either still tied to his mother's apron strings or he is emotionally immature. It is hard for a Christian wife to make a boy-husband a man-husband after he is twenty-one years old. In fact, around forty years of age, many of us who are men enter a second childhood called the male menopause. If you are married to a boy, seriously ask God for permission to shake the dust off your feet, preserve your dignity, uphold your virtue, and to remember how God honored the Virgin Mary. Prayerfully and courageously take God as your husband; leave that boy-husband, and let God help you rear up your children in a Christian home.

Girls, teenagers aspiring to be mothers, and you women: *Now* while you are in school, not later, get the best education possible. If your husband dies, has a tragic accident, or leaves you, your education will give you security, independence, and respect.

Fathers, husbands, sons, daughters, children: Please give mother a break. Don't smother her with too much love. She needs time to herself. She needs privacy. She needs rest. She needs a day off from housework. She needs a show, matinee, or a day to window-shop. She needs you to pick up your dirty socks. She needs you to wash the water glass after you drink out of it. Mother needs you to clean the dirty ring from around the bathtub, after your bath. Mother gets sick and tired of

29

being sick and tired, of hearing you children arguing, fighting, lying, and forgetting to make good on your promises never to do it again.

Daddy, walk the floor, if mama is late some nights in coming home. Walk the floor only if you are afraid that she has had trouble. But when she walks into the house, don't wake up the children fussing. Just ask the Lord to help you say: Welcome home, dear.

Children. Fail in school. Get in trouble with the law. Leave the house dirty. Stay out late at night. If you do these things, you will break your mother's heart.

Youth:
You can shorten mother's life by increasing her worries.

Young married child:
You can rush your mother to the grave if you run home every time you and your mate have a serious argument.

Husbands:
You can kill your wife by leaving the correcting of the children to her, and by criticizing her when the children turn out to be failures. Don't criticize the woman all the time. She *must be* worthy of praise sometime. Balance criticism with praise. Praise makes her a better person.

Now, let me conclude with our church covenant. It says "to religiously educate our children." Mothers, do you:
1. *Teach* your children God's word?
2. *Teach* your children how to pray?
3. *Know* if your child has a good Sunday-school teacher?
4. *Know* if your church has adequate space, staff, faith?
5. *Know* if the church library is adequate?
6. *Know* if your child eats in the sanctuary, drops candy wrappers on church property, and talks while the worship service is occurring?
7. Mothers, have you led your children to accept Jesus Christ as Lord and Saviour?

Do You Have a Dime?
(II Kings 4:1-7)

She didn't have a dime. She was born poor and married into poverty. What her name was we are not told. No knowledge is ours as to the names, ages, and sex of her two children. Unknown is the length of her marriage or which one of the sons of the prophets was her husband. All we know is that her poor seminary-student husband died leaving behind no insurance, but unpaid bills, and a host of unfriendly bill collectors. Isn't it a wonder that this woman did not soon follow her husband in death? But no, she faces Elisha, the president of the seminary, with her sad story.

Dried tears had left salty streaks on her face. The sad music of a broken heart used her feminine voice as a microphone. Her eyes no longer sparkled with hope, but were cloudy with discouragement. Doubt slowed her quick and graceful gait. Gloom pushed the sunshine of enthusiasm out of her life.

Hear this woman speak to Elisha in verse one: "Thy servant my husband is dead; and thou knowest that thy servant did fear the Lord: and the creditor is come to take my two sons to be bondmen."

Let us analyze these words. "Your servant my husband is dead. You know that my husband your servant feared the Lord, but the creditor has come. . . "

1. *First of all,* no matter how much you love the Lord or how much your mate or loved one loves God, death is coming. Saints die just like sinners. Have you made your preparation? Do you have insurance for burial? Don't

put it all in the ground. Leave some for your family to live on. A big expensive funeral is not an expression of Christian stewardship.

2. *Secondly,* no matter how much you love God, the creditor will come to take away your good name. You may be poor but you can have an honest name. If you are going to miss a payment or be late in paying, tell the creditor.

3. *Thirdly,* a close and careful examination of this text reveals that this young preacher left his tender and loving wife in the hands of a cold and cruel creditor who wanted blood itself. His good wife was in the hands of an evil man. If you would die, whose hands would your wife and children fall into? What protection do we have for our families? What kind of creditors do we do business with?

   a. Do we visit the loan shark?

   b. Do we know about low-interest loans from credit unions and banks?

   c. Do we stay away from high-interest-charging loan companies?

   d. Do we waste our money and then expect God to bail us out after we misused those blessings he gave to us? We need to save something out of each pay check.

   e. When we borrow from friends, do we pay them back so that they will help us or our children or our grandchildren far down the pathways of the future?

4. *Fourthly,* verse two explains that when Elisha heard her cry, he helped the young woman. Elisha ordered this widow *to borrow* vessels to fill with oil only after he discovered that although she had no dime—she had a jar of oil. When she got the vessels from the neighbors into her home, the jar of oil flowed freely into the other vessels. From the sale of oil, her bills were paid. From the sale of oil, she and her sons had money for living.

What is the message of this text? The text is telling us three things:

   a. Live so people will trust us enough to help us, and

   b. Before we give up, we must check our own assets.

"God has given each of us a jar of oil." Don't quit. Check your assets.

c. God expects Elisha and the neighbors to help. Elisha represents the ordained Gospel preacher and pastor. Ministers, we must get involved not only in heavenly matters of prayer but also in the dirty here and now of economics.

5. *Fifthly,* as a pastor, I am concerned about our use of money. Money, if used properly can pay for hospitals or if misused pay for honky-tonks. Money, if used in the right way, can pay for missionaries of God or, if misused, pay for missiles of destruction. Properly used, money can make a person generous of soul and liberal of heart. Wrongly used money can leave one bitter, selfish or sarcastic.

What does your money do? Does it bless or curse?
Does your money beautify or uglify?
Do you have a dime to build up East Oakland?
Do you support minority business in Elmhurst?

a. A church member owns Dixon's Fish Market.
b. A church member owns Jennifer's Ice Cream Store.
c. A church member and his wife, also of our Allen Temple family, own the restaurant at Apartment C.
d. Church members own real estate buildings on 14th Street and many real estate businesses are owned by Allen Temple members.
e. Don't buy what you can't afford.
f. Don't buy what you can't eat. That is wasteful behavior.
g. Don't look to HUD, HEW, the USA Labor Department, the President, the Governor, the Mayor or the City Council, Ron Dellums, Pete Stark, Fred Cooper, Leo Bazile or anyone else, to do for us in East Oakland what we must do for ourselves.
h. What if we stopped shopping at stores that refused to sweep their sidewalks? What if our church led a crusade to convert men who loaf, drink beer, and misbehave in public view on East 14th Street? What if

we had preaching services on the streets of East 14th?

i. When a white business leaves our community instead of setting up a new store front church, can't we pool our money and start up a business that will provide jobs for our own youth? Too many Allen Temple youth graduate from college and move to other places because we cannot hire them here.

j. Can you spare God a dime? Keep ninety cents of every dollar. God only wants a dime.

The Internal Revenue Service takes more money from us than what you and I give to God. When I ask for money or when other ministers ask for money, people accuse us of robbing them to line our own pockets. No, God's preachers speak for God. We merely remind people that God asks for at least a dime of every dollar. The issue is that the preacher has divine orders to preach the whole Gospel, not just what Gospel people want to hear. If the messengers preach the word, then God feeds, clothes, and cares for His messenger. Why criticize the preacher and leave the IRS untouched?

1. Don't forget that IRS collects your money to support CIA assassination plans around the world.

2. IRS money is used by the USA to support American interests in racist South Africa.

IRS uses your money to support an oppressive military economy. I am not a pacifist. I believe in self-defense. I believe in a diversified economy, rather than a single national economy that is built on the military industrial complex. I believe that God is not pleased with any economy that places more value on wishes than on needs or more value on things than on persons. I am convinced that our inflationary, materialistically oriented economy, where the rich get richer and the poor get poorer, is headed toward greater debt and the final destruction of America. No enemy from the outside will destroy this nation. From the inside, our wasteful habits will cause our demise. But—we don't have to die as a nation or as a race of people. *We can change.* We can teach our children new values and spending habits. We can teach them to give God a dime of each dollar. "One tenth for the Lord and nine for you.

It isn't so very much to do. And perchance the tenth may soon come back in heavenly favor; so where's your lack?''

Join the Tithers' League. If God gets His, and I get mine, then everything will be just fine. . .

"Will a man rob God, surely not! Robbed me? What do you mean? When did we ever rob you? You have robbed me of the tithes and offerings due me. And so the awesome curse of God is cursing you, for your whole nation has been robbing me. Bring me all the tithes into the storehouse so that there will be food enough in my temple. If you do, I will open up the windows of heaven for you and pour out a blessing so great you will not have room enough to take it" *(Living Bible—*Malachi 3: 8-11).

I hear God and angels discussing how Christians are obeying Malachi 3: 8-10, since they now have it in the *Living Bible* translation. Angels report to God:

1. *Roman Catholics* still obey, but not as much. They still have enough money to support Catholic charities.
2. *Mormons* are doing exceptionally well. They have large businesses such as Marriott Hotels.
3. *Jews* have enough money in Zion's treasury to force former Baptist President Jimmy Carter to lean closer to the small state of Israel than to those large Arab nations whose oil prices inflate American economy.

God asks about those Baptists. An angel says white Baptists do a fair job. They support evangelism, missions, and Christian higher education. But those black Baptists, some eight million of them in three national conventions are not doing so well. Yes! God, you heard right! Three conventions instead of one strong black convention to shake off the shackles of racism as did Moses and the Israelites in Egypt land.

Well—God—it's because too many want to be president. That's why they are divided.

Yes—God, it is a Satanic trick to divide among themselves and to fight each other. Yes—God, it is a waste of economic resources, and a waste of brain power, and prayer power.

But God—there is hope in Oakland at a church called Allen Temple. There your preacher is seeking to be Holy Spirit led.

FOR THE FACING OF THIS HOUR

There the members are learning to hear the word more and more. There the folk don't want to rob you. There for you they have a dime!

Telling the Good News to the Weak and Defeated

(John 4:1-31)

*Preached to The Annual Meeting
of Progressive National Baptists,
The Shrine Auditorium,
Los Angeles, California, August 1978*

Our Lord had spent nine months of successful ministry in Judaea. His astounding success attracted large crowds, and His disciples baptized far more converts than John the Baptist and his disciples. This success made the disciples of John jealous and it brought on increasing animosity from the Jewish leaders. Because of jealousy and hatred, it seemed wise for Jesus to move northward into Galilee. The most direct route was through Samaria. While most Jews took a winding and twisting snakelike route around Samaria, our Lord took the most direct route. It took Him straight to a village named Sychar. Near this place was a famous well built by Jacob, the Jewish patriarch.

It was noon on that winter day when Jesus approached the well. Finding the shade convenient, the Saviour rested while His disciples went into Sychar for food.

Shortly, a woman from Samaria showed up at the well with a water jar on her head, and a long cord to let the jar down into the well. It is conjectured that since the woman was in ill repute among the women of the town, she came for water at a time when the so-called good women would not be there.

FOR THE FACING OF THIS HOUR

There is a striking contrast between this woman and Nicodemus as recorded in the third chapter of John's Gospel. The fact that we have the name of Nicodemus in the Biblical record and no name for the woman reveals something of the low status of this woman. Even low status Jewish women were mentioned by name in the sacred Scriptures. But Jesus didn't discriminate. His good news is for both the strong and successful. Nicodemus was a respected Jew. This woman was a hated Samaritan. He was a man; she was a woman or a second-class, discriminated person in chauvinistic Biblical society. Nicodemus was learned; she was ignorant. Nicodemus was morally upright; she was immoral. Nicodemus was wealthy and from the upper class of society; she was poor and belonged to the bottom class. Nicodemus recognized Jesus' merits and sought Him out; she only saw Jesus as a hated Jewish male. Nicodemus was serious and dignified; she was flippant and boisterous. What a sharp, striking contrast between two people.

Yet Jesus did not discriminate. He was as kind and gentle to that woman as He was to Nicodemus. You see, the Gospel is for the weak and defeated as well as for the strong and powerful.

Jesus spoke kind words: "Give me to drink." She was scornful. "How is it that thou, being a Jew, askest drink of me, which am a woman of Samaria?" She gave Him water after she stung Him with piercing words!

Jesus didn't get angry. No, He didn't lose His cool. "If thou knewest the gift of God, and who it is that saith to thee, Give me to drink; thou would have asked of him, and he would have given thee living water. . ." Jesus teaches us that we are not responsible for scornful action of foes, but we are responsible for our reaction.

Jesus aroused her curiosity. He teaches us to be calm and to arouse the interest of those whom we wish to tell the good news. Notice the woman's curiosity.

"Sir, thou hast nothing to draw with, and the well is deep; From whence then hast thou that living water? Art thou greater than our father Jacob, which gave us the well. . ."

In order to increase her curiosity and to sharpen her appetite for the good news, Jesus appealed even more strongly to her desire. "Whosoever drinketh of this water shall thirst again: But whosoever drinketh of the water that I shall give him shall be in him a well of water springing up into everlasting life." "Sir, give me this water, That I thirst not neither come hither to draw."

This woman had an understanding problem. She was a materialist. All she could think about was water to satisfy her physical desire. This woman was thinking of economic values. Jesus was thinking of spiritual values. She was scornful, materialistic, and immoral. Racism had made her scornful. Chauvinistic men who had exploited her body made her materialistic. Jesus tore down the barriers of racism and sexism, and proceeded to build her up morally with proper self-esteem. He proceeds by saying: "Go, call thy husband, and come hither." Her answer was, "I have no husband." Jesus completely took the covers off the woman, saying: "Thou hast well said, I have no husband: For thou has had five husbands and he whom thou now hast is not thy husband. . ."

Like most of us, she put up her defense by changing the subject. She knew that she had been exposed so she changed the discussion to the topic of worship. "Sir, I perceive that thou art a prophet," the woman said. "Our fathers worshipped on this mountain; and ye say that in Jerusalem is the place where men ought to worship."

Jesus taught her that worship acceptable to God is not a matter of place. True worship is not a matter of time or space. Worship does not depend upon buildings and altars. Worship is not audience entertainment for those who expect the sanctuary to be a religious Circle Star theater. Worship recognizes that God is spirit; and they that worship Him must worship Him in spirit and truth. Worship is an act of personal commitment to God. Worship is also our collective commitment to God. After Jesus set the woman straight on worship, the woman saith unto him: "I know that Messias cometh." Jesus said unto her: "I that speak unto thee am he."

FOR THE FACING OF THIS HOUR

This is the first recorded disclosure of Jesus as Messiah. He didn't give His secret to the religious leaders or to the wise and powerful. No, He did not give this secret to theologians; He gave it to a Samaritan woman who opened both the mind and heart of Jesus. The response that this woman made to Jesus' self-revelation as Messiah is one we must remember. Her response made her do two things.

She left her heavy waterpots. No longer did she carry the heavy waterpots of guilt and self-rejection. No longer were her stops weighted by the heavy waterpots of sin. Now she had replaced guilt with the living water of joy and self-acceptance. Now, instead of carrying on her head the heavy waterpots of sensuality; she carried within her heart the living water of spirituality.

She left her waterpots. She left them without looking backward in remorse or regret. She left them without a longing for her past. She had no desire to drink the water of her Samaritan religious rituals. The age-old waterpots of custom and culture were to be left behind forever.

New water that brings new attitudes, new water that brings new purpose for living, new water that brings the sparkling taste of eternal life into the stale sameness of human existence, new water that makes one alive and related to a living Christ became the possession of this woman. New water was hers that came from her newly found Saviour. New and living water motivated this woman to leave where she was in order or to help to bear and share the good news to the town. She went into the city bearing good news to share. She told everyone what she saw.

"Come, see a man, which told me all things that ever I did." The New Testament Greek for this saying is, "Come see a man who understands me in a way no one else understands me." He understands me because He is able to enter into our pain. He understands me because His shoulders are broad enough to carry our burdens until our strength is sufficient to shoulder them ourselves. When the storms of life are raging and our lives are being dashed upon ragged and jagged rocks, the God who understands me will be there to console and caress me.

He has given me a story to tell and I must tell it to the nation.

I know the towns, hamlets, and villages of this nation. The Jesus story needs telling. Let us spread it to the dry deserts of the inner city. Let us spread it to the wastelands of city governments. Let us spread it to the barren terrain of our school and college classrooms. Let us spread it to the parched ground of residential communities. Let us spread it to people who are living in spiritual drought.

Yes, telling the good news is courageous work. It is difficult work. It is dangerous work. We may tire along the way. We may suffer setbacks. We may experience more failures than success. But we will not quit. We may find ourselves unable to move forward. Forces of evil may stop us in our tracks. But when that happens, we shall wait for the Lord.

"Why We Can Wait!"
(Isaiah 40:49-31)

Dr. Martin Luther King, Jr., wrote a powerful and persuasive book named "Why We Can't Wait!" In his book he told America that too long minorities and the poor have waited for justice. Long overdue was the banquet of brotherhood America had promised all of her citizens. For the sake of the dignity and destiny of the nation and the world, Dr. King felt that we could no longer wait for the nation to make good on the promises of the constitution. Since the death of Dr. King, the discriminated, despised and degraded have cried to the cold and comfortable: "We can't wait for the heat of love to warm your hearts."

I do not disagree with Dr. King. I believe that we can't wait for God to make our world better. We must work to help God make the world better by becoming better persons. However, there are some things that we obtain in life only by creative waiting. Waiting creatively upon God is one of them. Let me argue with you the reasons for my point of view.

Graduation from school does not prepare people for life. Certificates of paper with degrees or other credentials may certify you to work within the system. But letters in front of or behind your name do not mean that you are ready for life or that life is ready for you.

Learning comes from books, but wisdom comes from experience. Experience comes from the school of hard knocks. The curriculum is waiting until wisdom has prepared you.

The teachers are self-discipline, personal sacrifice, and unexplained suffering. The examinations are tears, trials, and tribulations. The freshmen class is failure, the sophomore class is disappointment, the junior class is doubt, and the senior class is determination. Patience is your post-graduate degree, and the ability to wait on God is your post-graduate doctoral degree. As you wait upon the fulfillment of your dreams, remember that creative waiting is preparation time for performing properly in a difficult and dangerous world.

Waiting Is a Maturing Time.
You do not pick cherries from the tree until they are ripe. You do not pick grapes from the vine while they are green. You do not pluck fruit from the tree until it is ripe. Sometimes we want God to do great things with us and for us before we are matured. It is dangerous to accept heavy responsibilities or difficult duties before we are ready. Sometimes we think we are ready when we are not. It is at these times when God slams the door of opportunity shut in our faces in order to give us waiting time for ripening and maturing. God did not build the universe in one day. He did the creation of these worlds in steps and stages. According to the Gospel of John, you and I do not see a completed world. In John, Jesus says, "My Father worketh hitherto, and I work. . ." Work prayerfully and patiently, but all the while wait for the maturing to take place. You can't speed up the pace of growth. Heaven has laws governing your growth. Creatively use your time of waiting to grow up a matured and seasoned person.

Waiting Is a Time of Building Readiness and Acceptance on the Part of Those Whom You Are to Serve.
You can't serve or help people if they are not ready to follow you. You can't lead people if their minds aren't with your mind. You can't give family, friends, or followers your vision if they don't dream your dreams. Sometimes, after you have prepared yourself, you have to wait until those you want to help are ready. A young man wooing a young woman for marriage may be ready, but if he is wise, he will not raise the

question of marriage, until she is ready. Prophets ought to move out in front to lead. But they must not move faster than the psychological and intellectual readiness of their followers. Sometimes waiting is a time for building readiness on the part of those you are to serve.

Waiting Is a Time of Self-Protection Against Haste and Waste.

Waiting is a time against careless rushing and haphazard preparing for a task. Waiting is insurance against shallow preparation. Waiting is an excellent defense against second guessing what God is going to do next. Waiting is security against blindly leaping into self-destruction. Waiting is a careful precaution against using the cash of choice for the first thing that comes along, and being embarrassed because your spent resources leave you powerless to purchase the best which is saved for the last. Waiting tells you not to change lanes on the freeway of life. For if you change lanes, the moving new lane will stop, and the lane you gave up will begin to move.

Finally, waiting teaches you to trust not your:
1. Academic preparation, nor your
2. Personal contact with powerful people, nor
3. Any other earthly source. . .

He gives power to the faint, and to him who has no might, He increases strength. Even youths shall faint and be weary, and young men shall fall exhausted; but they who wait for the Lord shall renew their strength.

Strength that you once had will be yours again!
Strength that brought you through the flood. . .
Strength that brought you across the desert. . .
Strength that brought you up, above, and across high mountains will be yours, if you wait upon the Lord.

If you wait for the Lord, you will mount up with wings like eagles and fly far above the storm. Yes, if you wait for the Lord, you will walk and faint not. The journey will not be too lonely or too long for you. Wait, and the living Christ will walk every step of the journey with you. Wait, and you will run and not be weary. When others tire in the race, when others drop out of the race, when others fall faint in the race, if you wait upon God, you shall renew your strength.

Wounded for Me
(Isaiah 53:5-6)

If God is responsible for all things, and since evil exists in the world, then is God responsible for evil? If God is not responsible for evil, how can God be a good God and allow evil to exist? Does the presence of evil in our world mean that God is helpless to change the world from a bad world to a good world?

If God exists and if He is so good, why do men seek to destroy each other? If God is good and powerful, why did He not change the trajectory of those bullets which killed John F. Kennedy and Martin Luther King, Jr.?

Let me answer these questions for you. Because God loved people, He made them to have freedom of choice. God did not make us to be dancing robots, or mindless puppets to be pulled by the strings of predestination.

God could use His power to twist human arms in order to make human beings behave in a moral way. But God has chosen to use not the power of force, but the power of persuasion. When God uses the power of persuasion, He is behaving in love. Force uses violence. Force is evil or destructive. Love heals, redeems, saves, allows us a new opportunity to correct evil behavior with morally responsible behavior.

Let us try to understand our responsibilities and God's responsibility for the evil in this world. Let us refrain from putting all of the blame on God. Let me explain my reasons for my plea to you. I shall try to do so by talking about sin.

The Bible speaks of personal sin and the sin of the world.

Personal sin lives in my heart and in your heart. It is jealousy, anger, pride, lust, and covetousness. It is as real as the birds of the air and the flowers of the field. The sin of the world means that outside of my heart and your heart, and separate and apart from your good intentions and my good intentions, and beyond your and my desire for goodness, an evil power is at work. There is evil in the human heart. There is also evil outside of the human heart. When our candle of goodness tries to burn brightly, the strong, invisible wind of evil blows it out so that people live in darkness rather than light.

God is a responsible God. Seeing us grope in darkness, He sent His Son, Jesus Christ as the light to save you and me individually, and to save the world collectively.

God as a responsible God is also a moral God. When you and I, and when the earth's first parents, violated the moral laws of God, a penalty was placed upon us.

If we face a penalty when we disobey man-made laws, if we even pay a penalty when we break a law as small as overtime parking at a parking meter, you can be sure that each one of us has to face the penalty for breaking the moral laws of God.

There we were, guilty before God, the judge of heaven and earth. There we were, guilty in word, thought and deed of breaking God's laws. There we were, facing the fact that in God's moral court of law: "The wages of sin is death."

Our own consciences had witnessed against each of us the testimony of **guilty.** Justice was our prosecuting attorney. Jesus Christ then stood up for us as our attorney. The court scene convened on a hill called Calvary. On that hill Jesus was pleading for you, for me, for all of us. He cried out, "Father, forgive them; for they know not what they do." Justice reminded God, the righteous judge that your sin, my sin, the sins of the world must be punished. You are stripped of human merit. I am poor in moral righteousness. All of us stood helpless and hopeless before a righteous Judge. Jesus, the attorney for all of us, played at this point a double role. The attorney for each one of us also became the bail bondsman for each of us.

Listen to Isaiah explain what happened on Calvary.

"But he was wounded for our transgressions, he was bruised for our iniquities: the chastisement of our peace was upon him; and with his stripes we are healed."

Wounded for me? Yes! The Christ is the one who suffers for me. He stepped into my place and accepted punishment which was meant for me.

Wounded for me? Yes! The innocent lamb of God gave me His innocence, and took on my sin, and became wounded for me.

Wounded for me? Yes! Millions and millions of people cover eternity as grains of sand on a seashore.

Yet, though I am a small speck of dust among millions and millions of persons from the past and present, it is true that "He was wounded for me!"

You ask, if God is responsible for all things, and since evil exists in the world, is God responsible for evil? I answer: A wounded Saviour got involved in the human predicament. A wounded redeemer confronted evil as our liberator. A wounded warrior stood toe to toe at Calvary with evil. There, heaven and hell had a contest. Darkness and light struggled each with the other. Error and truth strove to outlast each other. Sin endeavored to outrun holiness. Evil thought that righteousness had lost the victory. A compassionate shepherd had become the bleeding lamb. At the ninth hour, this champion of humanity bowed His head, uttered, "It is finished!" His head fell to His chest. It was the end.

Where was God when goodness was slaughtered?
Where was God when error knocked the under-
pinnings from under truth? Where was God
when sin stung holiness with the sting of
disgrace?

Don't panic? Don't fear? Don't lose heart!
Early the third morning a grave opens. . .

The slain lamb becomes
The risen Lord!
The Saviour powerless to save Himself
from the cross becomes the alive keeper
of the keys to death, hell, and the grave.

The wounded Saviour becomes the lamb
worthy of riches, glory and honor.

You critics of the faith, you ask if God is not responsible for evil, how can God be a good God and allow evil to exist? Does the presence of evil in our world mean that God is helpless to change the world from a bad world to a good world? God's wisdom answered you before the morning of creation. Listen to wisdom speak of our responsible God. Says wisdom: Let God become a Jew, a poor black Jew. Let Him be born in one of the smaller exploited countries of the world ruled by the iron hand of some great foreign power. Let God experience persecution, poverty, discrimination, prejudice and oppression. Let God be possessed with a great idea about the kind of world in which men ought to live, and let Him teach His ideas to the people of His own group. Let God be betrayed by those who profess to love Him, and be forsaken by His closest friends when He is caught in the iron vise of the governmental rulers of His day.

Let God be condemned unjustly and the verdict of guilty be pronounced upon Him. Let a cross be placed on His back, and let Him be whipped up some hill and suffer the most excruciating death that man can devise—crucifixion. Let God be nailed to that cross, and hang between heaven and earth, deserted, forsaken and alone. Let Him die there, *alone, alone, alone*. And God did what wisdom asked. He sent Jesus, who got involved in this evil world, even unto His death at Calvary.

Yes, I must preach this message of the wounded healer. He was wounded for my sins. He was my hero who won for me a bloody battle at Calvary. Bruised, beaten, battered, the bleeding elder brother named Jesus, stood in my place to do for me what I could not do.

> O wounded healer: You cleared my name!
> You cancelled my debt!
> You cleaned up my heavenly credit rating!

O carpenter Christ, with your wounded hands, you have prepared an eternal home for me. With the blood from your wounded side, you have purchased a transportation system to cross me over from time to eternity. At Calvary when a thief cried out in a dying hour, "Lord, remember me when thou comest into thy kingdom," your voice cried out, "To day shalt thou be with me in paradise." Lord, you then beamed home with your heavenly electronics a message ordering a two-seated chariot. "Father, I am coming home. I am worn and weary, but I am coming home. I am weak and wounded, but I'm coming home. Tell angels to send me a two-seated chariot. I am bringing home a converted thief who realized that I was wounded for his transgressions and bruised for his sins."

Were His wounds for you? Have you accepted Him and His salvation? Do you have time to accept today His salvation?

Missionary Obedience
(Matthew 28:19-20)

I have a very simple message today. You have heard this message. It is not something new. The message is so simple that you can ignore its truth in search of something that is more profound or intellectual. Let me say with emphasis that we miss the meaning of the simple because the simple is always with us, and we forget that which is with us in pursuit of that which is unknown or new. Take, for example, water. It is so simple that the value and purpose of water is fully appreciated only when rivers and reservoirs dry up and famine and drought stalk the land. In the land without water, the millionaire is as poor as the pauper. The desert treats with equal punishment both the millionaire and the pauper, the learned and the illiterate, the brown, black, yellow and white races, the young and the old. Says the desert, "Did you not know that you cannot cross these burning sands without water?"

But how simple water is. How little do we value or treasure water! It is something we take for granted! Let us not miss the simple in our search for the profound.

My simple message to you is that Baptists believe, and I hope, other Christians also, in the missionary task of making Christ known as Saviour and Lord. This is not saving the world. It is evangelizing the world. Missionaries cannot save the world. It is Christ that saves.

Science can build a neutron bomb which destroys people while preserving property. Science cannot save. Mathematics can teach persons to build computers and to calculate

51

thousands and millions of dollars. But mathematics cannot redeem persons from fraud, bribery, and theft. Grammar, speech, and composition can train the mind and lips to speak correctly, artistically, musically, and rhetorically; but is powerless to make the orator and poet a speaker of truth rather than falsehood. Medicine can repair the heart, and in rare instances, replace the heart. But medicine has no surgical skills to change an evil heart into a loving heart.

Psychology can master the mechanics of the human mind with psychiatry, but it is helpless in saving the mind from the sinful clutches of temptation or the destructive grasp of cruel thoughts. Money can purchase necessities and benefits for this life, but money cannot cure a broken heart, nor can money bring back from the silent halls of death a loved one, a revered family member, or a dependable friend! Law that punishes the criminal is powerful in judgment but powerless in redeeming the criminal from a career in crime. Law that tells a man he is wrong when he beats his wife, is helpless in enabling that man to love his wife. The United Nations, as effective and necessary as it is, has not discovered the peace formula for Arab and Jew, Dutch South African, and black African, whose oppression by Dutch South Africa is subsidized by American business interests.

Culture, civilization, and creative genius which flow from the river of human history has failed to save the world. But what culture, civilization, and creative genius can't do, the living Christ will do. Christ will save, if we will allow Him to be both our Lord and Saviour.

Our missionary task is to take the message of salvation in Christ to each and every slice and segment of human society. This means that we must know clearly where our mission field is. Where do we begin in the proclamation of the missionary message? Let us start first of all in the home.

The Family

How Christian is your home? Are prayers said aloud in your home? Is the Bible read aloud in your home? Is Christianity practiced in your home? Do *you* talk to unsaved persons in your family about Jesus Christ? Are you teaching your children to respect and honor you, themselves, others, and above all God? Teach your children to pray. The home is a mission field!

The School

If the home is a mission field—and I believe that it is, because in the home Cain still destroys Abel, in the home, Adam and Eve still permit the serpent to mislead them—then the next mission field beyond the home is the school. At school, satanic forces discourage Christian teachers and demoralize Christian administrators. At school, evil forces make it almost impossible for serious students to learn up to the level of their capacity. On Wednesday, April 26, 1978, at the Paul Lawrence Dunbar Elementary School, a fifty-six-year-old grandmother pulled a revolver from her purse and killed a thirty-eight-year-old janitor. She did the killing because the janitor had spanked her grandson. The grandson was guilty of bending the janitor's car antenna. Sin destroyed reason, and lighted the candle of anger in the grandmother, causing her to run to the school in a house dress, and her hair in curlers. She left a trail of blood in a school that will scar and harm the memory of her grandson far more than the sensations of a spanking. Drugs are sold on some school playgrounds as if they were competing with the neighborhood drugstore. Gambling in locker rooms, hallways, playgrounds, and on street corners by young people causes California to compete with Reno, Tahoe, and Las Vegas, for leadership in gaining a few dollars at the expense of others losing many dollars. The school, as well as the home, is a mission field.

The Neighborhood

Thomas Carlyle said, "Make yourself an honest man, and then you may be sure there is one less rascal in the world." Instead of heeding the voice of Carlyle, many persons, young and old, are hearing the voice of crime. Will Rogers phrased it correctly in saying, "We don't seem to be able to check crime, so why not legalize it, and then tax it out of business." If we could tax crime out of business then streets would be safe and homes would be secure, and rascals would be less. If we could eliminate cat burglars, then you would not worry about people breaking into your home during the day or at night while you are in bed, attempting sometimes, but succeeding most of the time, in stealing your hard-earned possessions. Let me tell you that the neighborhood is a mission field. The jungle where missionaries are needed is not only in Central Africa or the Amazon of South America. Your neighborhood is an asphalt jungle sorely in need of the Gospel. While evangelizing the East, Western culture must remember to evangelize her East 14th Streets, her Harlems and Watts. While the Gospel must be preached to the nations, you and I must preach it to our neighborhood. Neighborhoods in Oklahoma City, Omaha, and Oakland need the Gospel.

How many of your neighbors are sleeping in or resting up from worshiping the Saturday night god of pleasure while you worship here today? How many of your neighbors watch your property while you are away? How many neighborly neighbors are in your neighborhood? Yes, the home, school, and neighborhood, are mission fields.

If you go abroad as a missionary, you need to know the language and culture of the country where you are to serve. You need to know the history, politics, economics, and religions of the people you are going to serve, if you go abroad as a missionary. This requires disciplined study, personal sacrifice, and consecrated living.

Can't you be a missionary here among persons who speak your language, whose culture, history, and economics are the same as yours? Can't you do missionary work at home, at school, and in your neighborhood?

Each person who is a Christian has been charged with missionary responsibilities. The question is: Will you and I respond to God's command with loving missionary obedience?

Baptist history teaches that as a denomination we believe and practice missionary obedience. Were it not for missionary obedience, John Clarke and Roger Williams would not have organized at Providence, Rhode Island, in 1619, America's first Baptist congregation. Were it not for missionary obedience, George Liele would not have organized the first African Baptist Church in Savannah, Georgia, in 1778, and in 1783 would not have sailed to Jamaica to organize Baptist work there. Were it not for missionary obedience, former slave Lott Carey would not have saved $850.00 to purchase his freedom and that of his wife and two children in order to do missionary work in 1821 in the West African country of Sierra Leone. Were it not for missionary obedience, in 1840, twenty-five years before the signing of the Emancipation Proclamation, black Baptists would not have organized their very first convention: The American Baptist Missionary Convention which was born in Abyssinian Baptist Church of Harlem, New York. Missionary obedience gave us schools such as Shaw University of Raleigh, North Carolina, Virginia Union University of Richmond, Virginia, Morehouse College of Atlanta, Georgia, and Bishop College of Dallas, Texas. Were it not for missionary obedience, the world would not have had historian Carter G. Woodson, educator Booker T. Washington, singer Marian Anderson, preacher Martin Luther King, Jr., businessman C. D. Pettaway, and missionary Nannie H. Burroughs, the first president of the National Training School for Women and Girls in Washington, D.C. Was it not missionary obedience that sent J. L. Allen from Washington, D.C. to the West Coast to organize churches like Allen Temple? Was not my grandmother obeying the great commission when on Wednesday evening she led me to the Lord?

The cry has gone out this morning for those who will do missionary work at home, at school, and in the neighborhood. The plea has been given to women and men, and to boys and girls who love the Lord to obey the missionary call. What are you going to do? Paul said, "I was not disobedient unto the heavenly vision." Isaiah said: "I heard the voice of the Lord, saying, Whom shall I send, and who will go for us? Then said I, Here am I; send me."

Where Are We Going?
(Genesis 12:1-4)

Introduction

Where are we going in our individual lives? Where are we going in our collective lives as a race, as a nation, as a civilization? Where are we going as a church? Are we headed in the right direction or are we drifting off course on a direction that will lead us to the point of destruction?

Are we living so rapidly until we don't know how we are doing and where we are going? Are our values spiritually rooted or are our values shallow and surface values that glorify and glamorize the pleasure-oriented, status-centered lifestyles advertised in Ebony and Jet magazines? Is our family life a senseless imitation of the middle class T.V. family called The Jeffersons?

Who sets the pace for our lifestyles? Where do we get our code of behavior? How much are we influenced by television commercials, newspaper advertisements, movie stars, and public figures who have no love for the teachings of sacred Scriptures?

Where are we going? Are we following the morals of the masses? Are we devotees of the customs of culture? Are we prisoners of the past? Are we plodding the path of popularity? What place does God's word have in our lives? What priority does God's will have in our personal lives, our family lives, our life, and our social, political and economic lives? Do we allow God's word to determine our attitudes toward persons, money, and things? Where are we going?

Where Are We Going?

Where ought we to go? What road should we travel? What changes should we make in the travel plans of our lives? How far have we traveled on the road of life? How many miles do we have left to travel? How many days, weeks, months, and years are left before our journey on this planet will be ended?

Who is following in our footsteps? Whom have we misled on this journey? Whom have we led down the straight road? When did we last check our road map to see if we are on the right road? Who leads us down the road of history? Are we human rats in the rat race to get ahead or are we strangers and pilgrims on earth in search of a better country? Who are we? Whose are we? Where did we begin? Where are we and where are we going?

We Do Not Know How Far We Are Going!

Andretta Fowler is a loyal and faithful Allen Temple member, a tither, a generous giver, a silent saint who is active in the young adult Sunday school class. She seldom misses the prayer meeting and Pastor's Bible class. Recently upon rising to go to work, she carried her Bible to her new job, planning to return to the prayer meeting and the Bible class prior to returning home. An unexpected illness attacked her at work, forcing her to a hospital bed at Alta Bates in Berkeley. You and I propose but God disposes.

A Stanford-trained psychologist who counsels in a Menlo Park health clinic came to me for pastoral counseling. A friend who was set to move into a new home and who was ready to begin a new career had choked to death on a wad of chewing gum leaving behind a husband and several small children. Where are we going? Well, we don't know how far we are going or if we are going any place.

But we ought to try to go forward rather than backward. In Spanish they say, "Vaya con Dios," Go with God! And this is what Abraham did. Genesis 12:1-4 says:

Now, the Lord had said to Abram, Get thee out of thy country, and from thy kindred, and from thy fathers house, to the Land that I will shew thee: And I will make

57

of you a great nation, and I will bless you and make your
name great so that you will be a blessing. I will bless
those who bless you, and curse him that curseth thee;
and in thee shall all families of the earth be blessed. So
Abram departed, as the Lord had spoken unto him; and
Lot went with him. Abram was seventy and five years
old when he departed from Har-an.

We Must Go from Our Country Without Hesitation or Reservation.

The call of God leads us away from the comfort of where we
are to the adventure of where God wants us to be. This is
always a painful separation. We hate to give up the customs
of country to try the untried and the new. But God's call must
be away from before it can be a call to.

Move away from selfishness to sacrifice. Move away from
sensuality to spirituality. Move away from self-centeredness
to service. Move away from stubbornness to sensitivity. Move
away from sordid speech to stainless speaking. Move away
from the stench of your mental and social environment to the
sublime peaks of serious lifestyles. Move away from sickly
and spineless cowardice to strong and steel-like character.
"Abram, your father Terah is dead. Move out of the slums of
Haran into the summit of a new adventure with me. I will
show you this land, Abram. Trust me, Abram. Move and I will
take you to this land. Obey me and I will give you this land."

Trust and Obedience Are Necessary if We Are to Receive the Revelations of God.

Like Abram, you and I get the road map for our lives only
after we move out on the promises of God. Fear says to God,
"Heavenly Father, give me the complete road map and then I
will move." God says, "My child, trust and obey me if you
would obtain my promises." Broken hearts, unfulfilled
dreams, empty hopes, and failure followed by failure occur
when God's people disobey and distrust God.

Where are we going? Is it down the road of disobedience
and doubt? Why did our fathers live in faith and die in faith

58

while only 41 percent of young blacks ever register to vote and only 30 percent ever vote? Are our children sons and daughters of doubt?

Why are young black men comprising 80 percent of those on death row awaiting capital punishment? These young black men were placed there for killing white men. Very few are given capital punishment for killing large numbers of black brothers and sisters. Why is black life so cheap? Why is your own middle-class black life so cheap to your uneducated, unemployed black brother who will kill you to get just enough money to buy another dose of cocaine? Is it because our prayerless homes and non-Biblically oriented public schools have raised modern pagans who have never been taught: Exodus 20:13, 15, 16, 17,

"You shall not kill

You shall not steal

You shall not bear false witnesses against your neighbor,

You shall not covet your neighbor's house, your neighbor's
  wife, or his manservant or maidservant, or his "automobile" or anything that is your neighbor's."

Deuteronomy 6:5,

"You shall love the Lord your God with all your heart, and with all your soul, and with all your might."

Where are we going if our youth are uneducated, unemployed, misguided morally, and poverty stricken spiritually? Where are we going if we are fragmented as a race, jealous of each other as adults, failures as effective role models for our youth? Where are we going as a nation if we ostracize Black Panthers, stigmatize the nation of Islam, and glorify racism at home and magnify oppressive dictatorships in South America, South Africa, and Southeast Asia? Where are we going as a church if our Gospel is cut off from the streets, barrios, slums, and country clubs of the needy and the greedy?

Where are we going if economics become Reaganomics instead of Christonomics? Christonomics demand that we feed the poor, care for our elderly, and turn our battleships into brotherhoods and sisterhoods, and our bullets and military bases into building a human community of peace and understanding.

Where are we going if we poison our water with nuclear waste, our air with acid rain, and our food with chemicals and preservatives that cause cancer? Where are we going if brothers in labor and brothers in management kill the economy with strike after strike, resurrecting that ancient bloody battle of Cain and Abel?

Were we not called to live better lives? Were we not called to be great people? God did not make us angels. But neither did He make us to crawl in dirt like snakes or to fight like dogs who walk on four legs. God gave each of us two legs, instead of four, so we could walk uprightly. God in Christ taught us to walk uprightly. This is good news. Hence:

We Can Become God's Good News People to a World Sick with Bad News. Let's Face the Future with Good News.

Our future on this planet has unlimited possibilities. We need not give up. We need not capitulate to the unruly forces of destruction in our midst. We can be a blessing if:

1. We act now, since we do not know how much time we have left to make our contribution to humankind before death claims us.
2. We realize that trust and obedience are necessary if we are to receive a revelation from God, and
3. We can become God's good news people to a world sick with bad news. God's good news people have the promise of Abraham which was given in Genesis 12:2.

"And I will make of you a great nation, and I will bless you and make your name great, so that you will be a blessing."

God also says: "Your greatness is not for your own ego satisfaction. Your greatness is not for your abuse and misuse of power. Your greatness is so you can be a blessing to others.

Remember I am your army and navy. I am your air force and marine corps. I will be your secretary of defense and your commander in chief. 'I will bless those who bless you, and him who curses you. I will curse, and by you all the families of the earth will be blessed' " (Genesis 12: 3).

Conclusion

What is our future? Where are we going? Will our next ten years be as fruitful as the last? I do not know, but I hope so. Will we lead our community into greater unity? I do not know! But I hope so. Will we outgrow our new physical plant? I do not know. But I hope so. Will we establish a Christian school, grades K-12, and will we build a Bible college for our missionary in Liberia? I do not know! But I hope so. Will we sponsor economic development on East 14th Street within the next ten years and provide jobs for our people? I do not know, but I hope we will try to do so.

Will we improve in our giving of tithes and offerings? Will we progress in volunteer service at the church? Will we become more living, forgiving, and unified? I do not know, but I pray to God that we will. Will we send out more young pastors and missionaries? Will we improve our national reputation of educating our youth? I don't know, but I hope so!

Beams of heaven as I go,
Through this wilderness below,
Guide my feet into peaceful ways,
Turn my midnights into days.

I do not know how long 'twill be
Nor what the future holds for me.
But this I know, if Jesus leads me,
I shall get home some day.

Oftentimes my sky is clear,
Joy abounds without a tear.
Though a day so bright begun,
Clouds may hide tomorrow's sun.

FOR THE FACING OF THIS HOUR

There'll be a day that's always bright
A day that never yields to night.
And in its light the streets of glory
I shall behold some day.

Harder yet may be the fight,
Right may often yield to might.
Wickedness awhile may reign,
Satan's cause may seem to gain.

There is a God that rules above,
With hand of power and heart of love.
If I am right, He'll fight my battle,
I shall have peace some day.

I do not know how long 'twill be
Nor what the future holds for me.
But this I know, if Jesus leads me,
I shall get home some day.

Religion: Destructive and Constructive
(James 1:26-27)

"Anyone who says he is a Christian but doesn't control his sharp tongue is just fooling himself, and his religion isn't worth much." James in Chapter one, verse twenty-six, according to the *Living Bible*/Paraphrased, is giving his definition of destructive religion. Many years before James wrote these words, according to the King James Version, the Psalmist gave his description of destructive religion.

In Psalm 55:21 he wrote of the hypocrite: "The words of his mouth were smoother than butter, but war was in his heart; his words were softer than oil, yet they were drawn swords." Because the Psalmist did not want destructive religion to govern his life, he prayed in Psalm 19:14: "Let the words of my mouth, and the meditation of my heart, be acceptable in thy sight, O Lord, my strength, and my redeemer." Destructive religion, according to the Bible, is the religion of the sharp tongue. It is the religion of the person whose words are smoother than butter and softer than oil but whose heart is as harmful as war, and whose heart is as hurtful as the cutting blades of sharp knives or drawn swords. Destructive religion is unacceptable in the eyes of God.

A careless word may kindle strife,
A cruel word may wreck a life,
A bitter word may hate instill
A brutal word may smite and kill.

FOR THE FACING OF THIS HOUR

A joyous word may smooth the way
And a gracious word may lighten the day.
A timely word may lessen stress,
A loving word may heal and bless.

The Apostle Paul in Romans 3:13-17 describes destructive religion. According to the *Living Bible,* Paul said of persons with destructive religion: "Their talk is foul and filthy like the stench from an open grave. Their tongues are leaded with lies. Everything they say has in it the sting and poison of deadly snakes. Their mouths are full of cursing and bitterness. They are quick to kill, hating anyone who disagrees with them. Wherever they go they leave misery and trouble behind them and they have never known what it is to feel secure or enjoy God's blessing." Anyone who studies what the Bible teaches about destructive religion will discover two important lessons. Lesson number one teaches that the person who has destructive religion is an unhappy person. Lesson number two teaches that the person with destructive religion destroys the happiness of others. This is a fact because misery loves company.
God wants you and me to be happy persons.

Life is too short to be sad in,
To carry a grouch or to be mad in.
'Tis made to be happy and glad in,
So let us be friends and be happy.

Friends are too scarce to be sore at,
To gloom and to glower and roar at.
They're made to be loved and not swore at.
So let us be friends and be happy.

Love is the store we should lay in.
Love is the coin we should pay in.
Love is the language we should pray in.
So fill up with love and be happy.

No person should live without love or without loving. Love

is the answer to destructive religion. Destructive religion is built on fear, distrust, and suspicion. Perfect love casts out fear. Constructive religion is a religion of love for God and other people.

In James 1:27 a simple and clear definition of love is given. According to the *Living Bible:* "The Christian who is pure and without fault, from God the Father's point of view, is the one who takes care of orphans and widows, and who remains true to the Lord—not soiled and dirtied by his contacts with the world."

The Bible teaches us two truths to remember:
1. Destructive religion emphasizes *creeds;* and
2. Constructive religion emphasizes *deeds.*

Doctrines ought to be backed up with doing. Praying and saying ought to be followed by doing.

Do something for somebody somewhere,
While jogging along life's road;
Help someone to carry his burden,
And lighter will grow your load.

Do something for somebody, gladly,
Twill sweeten your every care;
In sharing the sorrows of others
Your own are less hard to bear.

Do something for somebody,
Striving to help where the day seems long,
And the sorrowful hearts that languish
Cheer up with a little song.

Do something for somebody always
Whatever may be your creed
There's nothing on earth can help you
So much as a kindly deed.
      Anonymous

In a conversation with my sister-in-law, she told me how she started visiting the elderly and the widows. She said she saw a sign at Pacific Care Convalescent Home while driving down High Street. It simply said, "Love is ageless. Come and visit us." Now she visits widows, orphans and elderly persons whom she does not know. This is constructive religion.

Neglected children await the loving attention of good religion. Boys who need a big brother because no man is present in their homes, hunger for the compassionate attention of constructive religion. Old persons in rest homes; senior citizens afraid of criminals in their neighborhoods; lonely persons at juvenile halls, jails and prisons; young people caught in a jungle of narcotics, neighbors starving for the gospel so that their souls can be fed, and former church members who have gone back to a sinful world—all need the understanding heart, patient ears, and helping hands of those with constructive religion. You ask me why you should practice constructive religion.

I know people are unreasonable, illogical and self-centered. Love them, anyway. Jesus did.

I know that if you do good, people will accuse you of selfish ulterior motives. Do good, anyway. Jesus did.

I know that if you are successful, you win false friends and true enemies. Succeed, anyway. Jesus did.

I know that the good you do today will be forgotten tomorrow. Do good, anyway. Jesus did.

People favor underdogs but follow only top dogs. Fight for some underdogs anyway. Jesus did. Ask the thief at Calvary.

What you spend years building may be destroyed overnight. Build, anyway. Jesus did.

People really need help but may attack you if you help them. Help people, anyway. Jesus did.

Give the world the best that you have and you'll get kicked in the teeth. Give the world the best that you've got, anyway.

God knows when you are doing your best. God sees. God hears. God knows. God understands. He will understand and say, "Well done, good and faithful servant."

Here I Stand
(Psalm 19:14)—(Job 19:25)

Heavenly Parent, whose Word to us became flesh in Christ, replace our hellish words below with heavenly words from above. Give us words not to accuse but speech to accept others as you have accepted us. May we not burn others with our words, but bless them with your message. Teach us to divest our vocabulary of words that cut, and to grow in the garden of speech words that console. Restrain our tongues from destroying others with destructive utterances. Drill us to discipline our talk with words that are dear. Instead of excoriating each other with terrible expressions, may we encourage one another. Instead of speaking falsehoods, give us fertile words of forgiveness to speak to each other. May we heal the hearts of the wounded with heaven's language of harmony, and not hinder the innocent with harmful talk. Teach us to inspire instead of injuring each other with our testimonies. In the name of the living Word, I pray, Amen.

When the room is crowded, or the bus or train is full, very few men will give up their seats to women. Even in a crowded church sanctuary, men are slow to give their seats to women or the elderly. Our generation prefers to sit rather than to stand. In our churches too many members sit on the premises instead of standing prayerfully on the promises of God's word. Sitting is easier than standing. Sitting is resting.

Standing is work. Many who sit enjoy allowing the evil meditations of their hearts and the cruel words of their mouths to condemn and criticize the sincere and best efforts of us who stand.

All standing is not good. Too many Christians, like Simon Peter, stand with the wrong crowd. Some try to stand on the sinking sand of neutrality. Some try to stand on the wet pavement of outdated tradition. Others dangerously stand on the weak floor of selfish and narrow thinking. Still others can't stand because they are slipping and sliding on the muddy surface of rumor and hearsay.

The year was 1963. The city was Oakland. The school was McClymonds High School. The students were seniors. The place was near Lake Tahoe. The season was winter. The unhappy ending of a beautiful beginning was death. A few students on a snow trip lost their lives. The thin ice upon which they stood gave way, and icy waters froze their bodies in a watery grave at the bottom of the lake. What are you doing? Are you sitting in a rocking chair of lazy religion or standing on the thin ice of criticism? Are you lounging in the easy chair of self-righteousness, or are you standing on the thin ice of absenteeism from Christian service?

In my message for today, I shall endeavor to tell you three things: 1) where I stand; 2) how I stand; and 3) why I stand. The title of the message, "Here I Stand," comes from Martin Luther. He nailed ninety-five theses on the door of the Castle Church in Wittenberg, Germany, on October 31, 1517. When asked to withdraw his criticisms on the shallow spirituality of the church, he answered, "Here I stand, I can do no other, God help me!" Not as Martin Luther, but as a sensitive Christian pastor I declare to you today: "Here I stand!" The four places where I stand are:

1. *Deeply cognizant of my own conversion experience.* The Holy Spirit has touched my life. I can truly say that I know Jesus Christ as my personal Savior and Lord. I can say with Paul: "If any man be in Christ, he is a new creature." We should strive to know Jesus not as a name, but as our personal Saviour. I stand also:

2. *Deeply conscious of my divine call to preach the unsearchable riches of the gospel.* I am more than a professionally trained preacher. The ministry is not a job or a means of a livelihood. For me, the ministry is a divine appointment. Why God did not bypass me and choose other more talented persons, I don't know. All I know is that when God called me, I was not disobedient to His voice. When the meditations of my heart kindle a flame of sacred love, I find that the words of my mouth struggle to preach their best. My call is to preach to persons of all races and groups of people. Thirdly, I stand here:

3. *Deeply committed to my commission.* Let the angry waves of opposition come. Let the flickering flesh of lightning disturb the sky of my emotions. Let the loud thunderclap deafen my ears so that I can't even hear God's silent voice reverberate within my soul. Let the demons of the devil pour down like raindrops upon my world so that my vision is blurred and my view is distorted. Let sinful storms bring hurricanes of discouragement and let the music of an evil wind sing disturbing melodies of falsehoods. I am deeply committed to my commission. For the Christ who called and commissioned me has said. Let the meditations of your heart remember my promise: "lo, I am with you alway, even unto the end of the world." Fourthly, I stand:

4. *Deeply committed to be constant in communion.* Prayer is my daily communion with God. In his book, *No Common Task,* George Reindrop describes a nurse who used her five fingers as a guide in praying:

Her thumb nearest her reminded her to pray for those near and dear to her.

The second or pointed finger reminded her to pray for her supervisors and leaders.

The third finger, the tallest reminded her to pray for the top leaders of governments.

The small fourth finger reminded her to pray for those who suffer from illness, disappointment and grief.

The little finger, smallest of all reminded her to pray tor herself.

Strong winds will keep you and me off balance, and will blow us off our feet, if we forget to pray.

Yes, I stand here cognizant of my conversion, conscious of my call, committed to my commission, and constant in my communion. How can I stand here? The Lord is my strength; by His power I stand. God's strength is my strength. He provides peace and power for upright posture in a chaotic and overpowering world. I stand here by the power of Jesus' ethical teachings as recorded by the Gospel writers:

1. Enemies are present, but Jesus says you lose if you fight them. "Love your enemies," and win. When you fight your enemies, you permit them to bait you, or to make you lose your cool head.
2. Do good to them who misuse you. Keep your hands clean. Keep your heart clean. Keep your mouth clean. Let the words of your mouth and the meditations of your heart be Christlike. If your enemies crucify you as they did Jesus, just remember that after the evil Friday of crucifixion, God always raises His sons and daughters on the third morning.

I stand here by the strength of Jesus' ethical teachings and by the power of Jesus' spiritual teachings. Hear our Lord's spiritual teachings:

1. "Lay not up for yourselves treasures upon earth. . ."
2. "Seek ye first the kingdom of God and his righteousness. . ."
3. "He that loveth father or mother more than me is not worthy of me: and he that loveth son or daughter more than me is not worthy of me. And he that taketh not his cross, and followeth after me, is not worthy of me. . . He that findeth his life shall lose it: and he that loseth his life for my sake shall find it."

FOR THE FACING OF THIS HOUR

Let us obey God's Word. The power to stand comes from obeying God's Word. God's Word commands us to love our enemies, to pray for those who despitefully use us. God's Word orders us to permit God's power to control the words of our mouth and the meditations of our heart. We disobedient children substitute our word for God's Word. We substitute our faith for faithlessness, the promises of God. When God calls, commands and challenges us, the meditations of our hearts, and the words of our mouth speak rebelliously to God. We secular-minded church members forget that God's work must be done by spiritually minded people. We trade the mind of Christ for the modern mind of logic and order. Our God is not a logical God. When God challenges us to trust and try Him, a worldly church questions the wisdom of God's ways. *Cowardice* among the members asks, Is it safe? *Tradition* within the congregation asks, Is it proven? *Greed* asks, Is it costly? *Doubt* among the church family asks, Is it practical? *Fear* asks, Is the time right? And a minority of folk called *dissension* ask, Is peace necessary?

My own mind is too small to question God. When He speaks I obey. His word becomes the words of my mouth and the meditations of my heart. His word tells me that the Lord is my *strength*. The Lord is my *redeemer*.

I would not be a Christian if God could not redeem me. A religion without redemption is a religion without salvation. A religion without salvation is a religion without good news. A religion without good news is a religion without hope. Hope is the promise of a better future. When hope dies, the pregnant mother of time dies with the unborn child of the future.

But our God redeems our future by redeeming our present. Let us conclude this message by seeing how God is our redeemer. God is the great physician of eternity. He enters the delivery room of time and assists the mother called *The Fading Now* into giving birth to a baby called *Almost But Not Yet*. He redeems the present and the future.

In the New Testament there are three words for Redeemer. They are:

1. *Exagorazo*. It means *to buy* a slave in order to free the

72

slave. Gal. 3:13 Paul reminds us that we were slaves of sin set free by Jesus Christ. The second word is:

2. *Lutroo.* It means to release on receipt of ransom. Sometimes a wealthy person will have a family member kidnaped, and will pay a ransom to free him. The third word:

3. *Apolutrosis.* Romans 8:23—I Cor. 1:30. It refers to the deliverance of the Christian from the presence and power of sin, and of his body from bondage to corruption, at the final coming of Christ.

In the Old Testament, Job used the word, *goel* for redemption. The *goel* was a family member who would vindicate your cause when you had been hurt or killed by a person of an unfriendly clan or tribe. Job 19:25, "I know that my redeemer liveth. . . ."

Church, State, and Regeneration
(Luke 20:20-26)

The earliest words spoken to us by Jesus Christ on church and state are our text words. "Render therefore unto Caesar the things which be Caesar's, and unto God the things which be God's." These words Jesus gave to His enemies, the chief priests and scribes. The sad truth is that both church and state joined hands to destroy the physical presence of Jesus. The state, following the leadership of organized religion, killed Jesus. But organized religion was unhappy with the title the state placed over Jesus' cross, THIS IS THE KING OF THE JEWS. It is the Gospel of John which informs us that the chief priests and scribes said: "Write not, the King of the Jews; but that he said, I am King of the Jews. Pilate answered, What I have written, I have written."

After the death, burial, and resurrection of the Christ, the Christian church enjoyed toleration from the state. According to the Book of Acts, the Christian church was persecuted by the Jewish church. It was the state that protected Paul from the persecution and hatred of the Jewish church. However, this protection was short-lived.

From tension to toleration, and from toleration to persecution, the Christian church moved in her relationship with the state. Around 111 A.D. Christianity was considered to be a criminal religion by the Roman state. The early Christians were charged with atheism and anarchy. Ignatius of Antioch, who was Bishop between 110-117 A.D. was thrown to wild beasts by Roman Emperor Trajan. Polycarp, Bishop of

74

Smyrna was burned at the stake in 156 A.D. An African named Cyprian, who was Bishop of Carthage, was beheaded in 258 A.D.

This conflict between the Roman state and the Christian church continued until it was curtailed in 260 A.D. by the edict of Gallineus. The Edict of Milan in 311 A.D. brought peace to the Christian church by the Roman state.

Church and state relations moved from tension, toleration, persecution, toleration the second time, to an unholy alliance in 323 A.D. under Roman Emperor Constantine. It was then the state co-opted the church for her unholy ends. Rome became known as the Holy Roman Empire, but there was nothing holy about the empire.

War, corruption, and moral degradation made up the unholy triad of the united church-state or state-church. Historians call these ugly years of the church "The Babylonian Captivity of the Church." This sordid and stained history of the world in the church was not broken until October 31, 1517. It was then Martin Luther nailed ninety-five theses on the door of the Castle Church of Wittenberg, Germany. This act gave birth to the Protestant Reformation, which in turn gave birth to the separation of church and state.

Of all the Protestant bodies in Christendom, Baptists, more times than can be counted, have led the movement for religious freedom or the separation of church and state. Baptists, influenced by Roger Williams and others, led Thomas Jefferson and James Madison to build religious freedom and the separation of church and state into the U.S. Constitution. The First Amendment to the Constitution declares that "Congress shall make no law respecting an establishment of religion, or prohibiting the free exercise thereof; or abridging the freedom of speech, or of the press, or the right of the people to assemble, and to petition the Government for a redress of grievances."

Why do we as Baptists believe in the separation of church and state? The church as used in this message is an inclusive term for all denominations that confess Jesus Christ as Saviour and Lord. Church, therefore, is capitalized; and churches, spelled with a small "c," make up the Church. State refers to any national government or to any recognized nation that has its own government. Now, back to our question: Why do we as Baptists believe in the separation of church and state?

1. First of all, Jesus in our text commands us to "Render therefore unto Caesar the things which are Caesar's; and unto God the things that are God's."

2. Separation means that the Church has a unique reason for being.

3. Separation means that the Church has a head separate and apart from the head of the State. The State's head is impeachable but the head of the Church is unimpeachable.

4. The Church has its own public. The State includes everyone that is born into its territory. The Church is for the second born or the regenerated. The second birth differs from the first birth. Under the second birth, you can choose whether you want to have spiritual regeneration. In the first birth you had no say.

5. The methods are different: the State legitimizes violence. The Church listens to God who says: "Not by might, nor by power, but by my spirit saith the Lord."

6. *Separate Administration Required.* The State, if it is a democracy, is ruled by the political party given the power by the masses. If it is totalitarian, it is ruled by those dictators in power. If it is an oligarchy, it is ruled by the wealthy. If it is a monarchy, it is ruled by kings and their heirs. The Holy Spirit is God's invisible, ruling presence in His Church. His churches are cared for by ordained, called ministers of God.

7. *Separate Sources of Support:*
   a. The State takes from her constituents tax money.
   b. God's Church depends upon the free-will tithes and offerings of the Christians. Gentiles are not to support God's work.

8. *Separate Educational Programs.* The church cannot delegate to Caesar the educating of her members. Did not

Jesus say: "Go ye therefore, and teach. . ." Yes, we
believe in the separation of church and state.
We believe that God wants the Church in the world, but that
He does not want the world in the Church. We believe that
when God and Caesar have a conflict in law or morality, we
must always obey God. We believe that Christians must be
citizens of two worlds.

Building a Usable Future
Creating a Usable Future

At the University of Southern California, in the office of my friend, Dr. Thomas Kilgore, Jr., I saw written above the desk of one of his secretaries, a sobering question. This startling question staggered my mind with these words, "Will it matter that I was?" Think about this simple question. Will it matter in ten years, twenty years, fifty years, one hundred years that you were? Does it matter now that you are alive? For my grandchildren, your grandchildren, and for grandchildren that are yet unborn, are you creating a destructive or useable future?

Economist Robert L. Heilbroner, in his book, The Future as History, says: "The future itself is a direction in which we look no longer with confidence but with vague forebodings and a sense of unpreparedness."[1] Our experiences tell us that Heilbroner has spoken the truth. Youth unemployment is high and among black youths it is incredibly high, perhaps 60 percent. Poor nations are becoming poorer; rich nations are becoming richer. High taxes, rising inflation, the flight of factories and businesses from the city to surburbia, the disintegration of family life, the increase of crime among the youth, and the decrease of respect for senior adults, the rejection of spiritual values for material values, the continuous cry for more—all this suggests that the future is a direction in which we no longer look with confidence.

Some of us have false hopes because we depend upon the passing of time to take from our eyes into the future present problems. Others of us have false despair for the future, which permits us to predict doom for tomorrow even before we try to create a useable future. Still others of us are too fearful to oppose the present evils that kill those gains of the past. Many a stride forward that was made by people like nonviolent leader Martin Luther King, Jr., is being erased from the footprints of history by black and white alike who worship the god of violence. A useable future cannot be created when ignorance is busy trying to turn the clock of history backward into the Dark Ages.

Ignorance sometimes wears a cap and gown from our best universities. Listen to Jean-Paul Sartre say, "Life is an absurdity." Listen to Martin Heidegger say that, "Man's existence is a being toward death." Listen to British scientists William Thomson and Lord Kelvin argue the entropy of energy, the doctrine that all energy burns itself out and hence social energy or moral goodness, like physical energy, will burn itself out. If I followed this line of reasoning, I would give up hope, saying that all I do for Christ is in vain.

From the false despair of scholars like Sartre, Heidegger, Camus, and a host of others, we go to the false hope of the renowned scholar-theologian Teilhard Chardin. Dr. Chardin argued that history is moving us from the cosmosphere (that is, inanimate matter), to the noosphere (that is animate matter), to the biosphere or human life to the Christosphere. Chardin overlooks the eternal dues the sinner must pay for his sinful collusion with evil. Chardin gives everybody salvation, neglects the individual, and places little value upon the present moment. Chardin treats the present as if it is only a minute second upon the clock of eternity. To personalize or to accept Chardin's view of the present will discourage one from trying to create a usable future.

The prophets of doom in our universities, in politics and in government are saying that there is nothing we can do to change history. We are on a destruction course. It is too late to turn back. Listen as the environmentalist speaks.

1. Through our rapidly increasing consumption of carbon-based fuels, such as coal, oil, gas, we release

such an amount of carbon dioxide into the earth's atmosphere that nature will no longer be able to balance this by using up carbon dioxide in plants and releasing the corresponding amount of oxygen. But who said that alternative energy sources could not be found? Already scientists are saying that in twenty-five years 25 percent of the earth's energy will come from the sun.

2. Prophets of doom are saying that regardless of our new agricultural methods, our ecosphere is able to support only six to eight billion people. But who said that the discipline of planned parenthood could not become an attainable reality?

Christianity is a religion which has hope in God who is the Alpha and Omega of human history. This deep and abiding faith grows out of a careful study of the Bible. Listen to our text, Hebrews 11:23: "By faith Moses, when he was born, was hid three months of his parents, because they saw he was a proper child; and they were not afraid of the king's commandment." In those days it looked as if Jewish boy babies had no future. In fact, it looked as if genocide as practiced by the Egyptians would erase from the blackboard of history, the future of the Jewish race.

The Jewish family has no logical or intellectual basis for survival. They were slaves in powerful Egypt. Military might, economic power, and scientific know-how were controlled by Egyptians. Centers of culture, institutions of learning, medical centers, leaders in the fields of labor, business, and the professions were all Egyptians. Jews were unlearned, unpopular, underdeveloped, and unwelcomed in Egypt. An evil Pharaoh was conducting a campaign to rid Egypt of a young and growing Jewish presence. But in this ugly and hopeless situation, two people with faith in God moved to create a useable future for their son named Moses.

This text tells us three simple truths. First, God used people to bring about change. Second, God used a minority of persons to bring about change. Third, God used a diversity of persons to bring about change:

Building a Usable Future

1. Moses' parents!
2. Moses' sister!
3. Pharaoh's daughter!
4. Pharaoh's servants!
   All helped to bring about change.
   (The place where you least expect help is from whence it always comes.)
   Help came from:
5. Jethro, who taught Moses the science of wilderness survival, and
6. Aaron, Moses' brother, who appears in the Bible only after reaching adulthood.
   Because of their faith, a useable future was created.

FOOTNOTES:

¹Robert L. Heilbroner, *The Future as History*, N.Y., Harper, 1960, p. 193.

Everyday Ethics: Challenge for Ministry

Presented: February 19, 1980 at the Christian Life Workshop, Southwestern Baptist Seminary, Fort Worth, Texas

Introduction: Theological Assumptions

I believe in Jesus Christ as the living lord of history and as the servant model for the servant-church. I believe that the church in the world is to continue the work agenda of our Lord in a servant ministry to a world in need of healing and reconciliation. I believe in the ability of the parish church to incarnate the heart and mind of Jesus Christ in action to humanize and personalize life in a dehumanized and depersonalized environment. I agree with Alvin C. Porteous in his book, *The Search for Christian Credibility,* that it is a misguided utopianism which gives up on the church simply because it exhibits no immunity from the distortions and frailities of other social institutions.[1] In addition to being a sociological community which reflects human imperfections, the church is a community that serves as "the salt of the earth and the light of the world." This could have been the partial basis of Abraham Heschel's words:

Man is a duality of mysterious grandeur and pompous aridity. A vision of God and a mountain of dust. It is because of his being an image . . . that his righteousness is expected.[2]

Because of human possibilities, and because the black church in America nourished us with courage when hope unborn had died, I say as the son of this church, that local congregations make a difference in the world when they have vitality and a deep sense of mission. In California many conservative churches who prided themselves on theological accuracy have cooperated with minority congregations only when they needed minority support in promoting evangelistic crusades by groups such as Campus Crusade for Christ. When racial minorities and the poor and elderly among us cried for help, Southern Baptist and American Baptist transitional churches, Presbyterians and so-called liberal denominations joined hands to support black churches in the liberation struggle. The black church on the whole has converted oppression into poetry, exploitation into creative force, humiliation into hunger for justice, haunting fears into hymns of faith.[3]

Black seminary graduates of the Associated Theological Schools' seminaries learn classical theological concepts but culturally are unable to understand majority group debates on the dichotomy between evangelism and social action. Jesus has taught us that there is no separation between happiness and heaven, hunger and hell, justice and justification. The lordship of Jesus Christ controls both our prayers and our purse. The sovereignty of God shapes the service of the church. These statements provide the ethical and theological basis of the outreach ministry of the Allen Temple Baptist Church of Oakland, California.

The Allen Temple Baptist Church Outreach Ministry

In November, 1970, the Allen Temple Baptist Church called me to serve as their pastor. The membership accepted my conviction that the Elmhurst community and the city at large must be our turf, and we agreed not to recoil from the problems in our neighborhood and in our city. In a ten-year period, the membership has grown to the extent that members drive weekly and bi-weekly from faraway places in the Greater San Francisco Bay Area in order to meet in the church buildings for the planning of ministry to the world and in the world. The first project that we as a church embraced was in the area of public education. With the leadership of professional educators and volunteers in the church, we developed strong tutorial programs.

1. *Tutorial Programs*
    a. Elementary school children, 3:15 to 5:15 P.M. Tuesdays and Thursdays
    b. Youth Tutorial Program, 7:00 to 9:00 P.M. Tuesdays and Thursdays. Courses taught by *Black Engineers Association.*
    c. College Entrance Examination. Board classes on Saturday mornings were designed to aid students pass PSAT, SAT and C.E.B. exams.
    d. Annual Job Fair and Career Day Conferences
    e. Annual Scholarship Sunday; $54,000 raised in 1979 for scholarships
    f. An Adult Day School under the leadership of Mrs. J. Alfred Smith, Sr., provides basic educational skills and English as a second language to all persons.
    g. Twelve young persons are preparing themselves for the Christian ministry as pastors; six other persons are working on degrees in Christian education.
    h. Merritt College offers college credit to students who enroll in the pastor's Bible Class.
    i. We sponsor Cub and Boy Scout troops.
    j. We have field trips and cultural enrichment programs to colleges and universities for youth.
    k. We have a youth ministries and youth representation on all boards and committees. The youth minister is J. Alfred Smith, Jr.
2. *The Health Field*
    a. We gave birth to the East Oakland Health Alliance, an autonomous community health clinic whose budget

is many times larger than our church budget. The clinic has a medical, dental and mental health division.

b. Allen Temple Counseling Center provides services free of charge to all who seek help.

c. Annual Health Fair, where high-blood-pressure testing and other programs give free medical examinations and counseling.

d. A Blood Bank provides services for all who can't afford to pay for blood.

e. An Athletic Department:
   (1) 16 Adult bowling teams
   (2) 3 baseball teams
   (3) 1 softball team
   (4) 1 swimming team
   (5) 1 women's exercise team
   (6) 1 basketball team

f. Annual Athletic banquet where professional athletes appear as role models.

3. *Economics*
   a. We have annual Money Management Seminars sponsored by the Junior Business and Professional Women.
   b. We have the Allen Temple Federal Credit Union for the membership.
   c. We have Benevolent Fund and Food Box for all needy persons.
   d. We sponsor a Mini-Mart Discount Food Center for all Senior Adults.
   e. We conduct a Job Information Center for all unemployed persons.
   f. We have a long range committee on economic development for our neighborhood and we have purchased commercial property for economic development.

4. *The Outreach into the Community is as follows:*
   a. The WIC Program for mothers designed to reduce infant mortality: Program for expectant mothers and

mothers with children under five years of age.
b. A Big Sisters' Program
c. A Big Brothers' Program
d. Juvenile Hall Ministry
e. Prison Ministry, and
f. a Comprehensive Crime Prevention Office at the church.

5. *Political Involvement*
   a. We sponsor Voter Registration at the church.
   b. District Election Advocacy and Candidate Nights at the church.
   c. The Christian Social Concerns' Committee monitors City Council, School Board, and County Supervisor's meetings. They hold those persons to a relative kind of accountability.
   d. We recruit Christians to run for public office.
   e. We are forming political coalitions with Hispanics, Asians, and Caucasians of good will.

6. *Neighborhood Revitalization Programs*
   a. We are sponsors of seventy-five units of elderly housing.
   b. We persuaded Clorox Company to build a 1.5 million dollar youth center.
   c. We persuaded Pacific Gas and Electric Company to locate office buildings in East Oakland for the elderly and poor.
   d. We are an advocate for housing rehabilitation now taking place in our community which suffered too long from "redlining" by all lending institutions and banks.
   e. We are responsible for the economic revitalization of the minority business strip in our Elmhurst district.

7. *Reconciling Action with:*
The Spanish-speaking community, the Black Panther Party, the Asian Community, and the Native Americans. Mr. and Mrs. Henry Woods serve as ministers to the Hispanics. Both are bilingual Hispanic persons within the membership.

8. *Leadership in Plant Closures Project*
   a. Advisory Board

> Harry Cahill
> Directing Business Agent
> International Association of Machinists
> District Lodge 115
>
> Thomas J. DiMaggio
> Sub-District Director
> United Steelworkers of America
>
> Richard Groulx
> Executive Secretary-Treasurer
> Alameda Central Labor Council
>
> Newton Kamakani
> Financial Secretary
> United Auto Workers Local 1364
>
> Curtic McClain
> Secretary-Treasurer
> International Longshoremen and
> Warehousemen's Union
>
> Chuck Mack
> Secretary-Treasurer
> International Brotherhood of Teamsters
> Joint Council 7
>
> Rabbi Sam Broude
> Temple Sinai
>
> Reverend Warner H. Brown
> Director, The Council on Ministries
>
> Reverend Doctor William Coleman
> Inter-Ministerial Alliance
>
> Father George Crespin
> Chancellor, Diocese of Oakland
>
> Reverend Eugene Farlough
> Pastor, Sojourner Truth Presbyterian Church

FOR THE FACING OF THIS HOUR

Reverend Mineo Katagiri
Conference Minister
Northern California Conference

Reverend Alan McCoy, O.F.M.
President, Conference of Major
Superiors of Men

Reverend Doctor J. Alfred Smith
Pastor, Allen Baptist Temple

John George
Alameda County Board of Supervisors

Elihu Harris
Assemblyman, Thirteenth District

Gertrude Hodges
Director, Progressive Black Business
and Professional Women, Inc.

Florence McDonald
Councilwoman, City of Berkeley

Robert Macias
Executive Director
Spanish Speaking Unity Council

Harry Polland
Economic Consultant

Wilson C. Riles, Jr.
Councilman, City of Oakland

Charles Santana
Alameda County Board of Supervisors

b. PLANT CLOSINGS: Who Loses?

[1] The Worker

Based on studies by Dr. Bennett Harrison of M.I.T. and Dr. Barry Bluestone of Boston College, plant closure victims take longer to find new jobs than workers laid off for other reasons. If they do happen to find a job, the pay is much lower than their pay was in their former job.

LENGTH OF TIME TO FIND A NEW JOB

Over 12 months	6 to 12 months	0 to 6 months
25%	15%	60%

49 weeks is the average time it takes for plant closure victims to find a new job.

PERCENTAGE OF WAGES COMPARED TO FORMER JOB

Industry Closing	After 2 Years	After 4 Years
Steel	54%	87%
Auto	57%	85%
Meat Packing	76%	82%

Particularly hard hit are workers over forty-five years old. Statistics kept at one large plant closing showed that after one year 65% of those workers over forty-five years old were still unemployed, compared to an unemployment rate of 30% for those under forty-five.

As workers get older problems with pensions represent a tremendous loss. Many workers go through more than one plant closing. Since pensions are not guaranteed by law until after ten years of service, many workers never qualify because their plants continue to shut down before they become eligible.

Minorities and women are especially hard hit by the failure to qualify for pensions. Recent affirmative action

89

gains are being erased. The situation facing many minorities and women is worse now than before they got their jobs. Urban areas showing minority youth unemployment rates of 30% and higher are a reflection of the larger impact of plant closures on our communities.

PLANT CLOSURES PROJECT
433 Jefferson, Oakland, CA 94607
(415) 834-5656

A study done by Dr. Harvey Brenner of Johns Hopkins University showed the following results for a 1% increase in the national unemployment rate:
- 37,000 total deaths (20,000 cardiovascular)
- 920 suicides
- 650 homicides
- 500 deaths from cirrhosis of the liver
- 4,000 state mental hospital admissions
- 3,300 state prison admissions

In Wilcick and Franke's study Unwanted Workers: Permanent Layoffs And Long Term Unemployment, increased health problems show in the following areas:

- Mental: sense of deprivation/ loss of self-esteem/ loss of self-identity/ loss of confidence; and feelings of uselessness.
- Physical health: increased likelihood of coronary disease; increased risk of diabetes, peptic ulcers, and gout. Increases were also found in arthritis, chronic asthma, kidney disease, respiratory disease, and skin disease.
- Family health: Increased infant mortality, pregnancy problems, malnutrition, sexual impotence, juvenile delinquency, divorce, and drug and alcohol abuse.

[2] The Community

When a plant shuts down the local community suffers terrible economic and social costs. Both property and retail sales taxes will drop. Increased social costs put a greater burden on community resources. Job loss does not stop at the one plant shut down either. THE CLOS- ING OF A MAJOR MANUFACTURING PLANT CAN CAUSE THE LOSS OF UP TO 3.5 MORE JOBS IN THE SUPPORTING PARTS, TRUCKING, RETAIL SALES, WAREHOUSING, AND PUBLIC SERVICE INDUSTRIES THAT SERVICE THE PLANT OR ITS WORKERS.

The community also suffers from the social impact of plant closings. In a study done of Coos Bay, Oregon, a community hard hit by lumber and mill closures, a dramatic increase in crime and social problems was documented. Despite a 9% drop in population between 1979 and 1980, the following increases in crime and family violence occurred during the same period:

- 31.3% increase in eight major criminal categories, in- cluding rape, homicide, robbery, aggravated assault, burglary, larceny, motor vehicle theft, and arson.

- Burglary up 42.6%, disorderly conduct up 29.8% and an overall increase of 14% in all categories of crime.

- A sharp rise in police calls involving domestic vio- lence.

- A 500% increase in clients at the local Women's Center that services emotionally and physically bat- tered women.

The Conclusion

The Allen Temple Baptist Church has a street evangelistic preaching team. There are revival meetings and evangelistic visitation. There are classes for new members on Christian discipleship. There are neighborhood Bible classes, but all of these activities seek to relate the dogma of Christianity to the day-to-day struggle of living. We do not believe in other worldly Biblical studies. We agree with Harvey Cox who said in *The Secular City*, that speaking about God must be "a word" about "peoples" lives—"their children, their job, their hopes or disappointments. It must be a word to the bewildering crises within which our personal troubles arise.... If the word is not a word which rises from a concrete involvement of the speaker in these realities, then it is not a Word of God at all but empty twaddle."[4]

"Now to Him that is able to do exceeding abundantly above all we can ask or think, by the power which is at work among us, to Him be glory in the church, and in Jesus Christ from generation to generation evermore" (Ephesians 3:20-21).

FOOTNOTES:

[1]Alvin C. Porteous, *The Search for Christian Credibility,* Nashville: Abingdon Press, 1971, p. 180.

[2]Abraham Heschel, *The Insecurity of Freedom,* New York: Farrar, Straus and Giroux, 1966, p. 158.

[3]Otis Moss, Jr., "Black Church Distinctives," pg. 15 in Emmanuel McCalls, *The Black Christian Experience,* Broadman Press, Nashville, 1972.

[4]Harvey Cox, *The Secular City,* The MacMillan Company, New York, 1965, p. 256.

The Church, Home Base
for Everyday Ethics

Presented: February 20, 1980
at the Christian Life Workshop,
Southwestern Baptist Seminary,
Fort Worth, Texas

What is Christian faith? Is it the conceptual affirmation of
creeds or the literal acceptance of articles of faith? Jose
Miguez Bonino confronts us with this question. He asks: "Is
the Christian faith the acceptance of the correct interpretation
of certain texts, or is the Christian faith the commitment to
obedience to the Lord Jesus Christ?"[1] If the question is the
latter, really, the question is, how does this obedience express
itself concretely, so that you really know how the text has to
be understood in relation to your total Christian experience.
So actually you cannot say whether you read the text correctly
until you say how you treat the poor farmer.

Academic persons should not fret over Bonino's words. No
attempt is made to deprecate serving God in a thoughtful
manner. What Bonino is attempting has best been expressed
by Gustavo Gutierrez and James Cone. Listen to Dr. Cone who
defines theology as "the rational study of the being of God in
the world in the light of the existential situation of the oppressed community, relating to the essence of the gospel
which is Jesus Christ."[2] Dr. Cone does not arrogantly define
the theological task from the angle of vision of the powerful in
God's household of faith. Gutierrez challenges the church and
each local congregation of Christ's body in his definition of
the church and theology.

Listen to his powerful words: "The Word of God is incarnated in the community of faith which gives itself to the service of humankind. This activity of the church as the community of faith must be the starting point of all theological reflection."[3] Finally, you and I need to pay attention to Hugo Assman who strikes the target with the arrow of truth in writing, "Faith is the action of love within history."[4]

I embrace these views of our mission in looking at ethics for every day. I do not believe that theology is merely philosophical exercise, mental jogging, intellectual Ping-pong, or the defining of orthodoxy as the rejecting of "your doxy" for "my doxy." I believe that theology is thoughtful Christian living. This thoughtful Christian living pushes us outside the wall of church sanctuaries into a secular society which does not understand the "shop talk of theologians" or the "secret society language of lay evangelists" who invade personal privacy with questions like: "Are you saved?" Moving out into the world, thoughtful Christians, endeavoring to live their faith, will meet the living Christ of history, who travels incognito, but who is always on the side of all persons who seek order in chaos, love amidst depersonalization, and justice where injustice reigns. "And His name shall be called Emmanuel, which means God with us" (Matthew 1:23b).

Our Asian Christians, doing theology from their third-world cultural perspective, understand this reality. Theology is a living experience with them. They cannot separate theology from ethics. Therefore they say: "We have had rice with Jesus."[5] In our own mind, it seems also logical for them to say, "We have been hungry with Jesus. We have been thirsty with Jesus. We have been cold and naked with Jesus. We have been despised and rejected with Jesus. We have been poor and neglected with Jesus."

"Who has believed our message and to whom has the arm of the Lord been revealed? He grew up before him like a tender shoot, and like a root out of dry ground. He had no beauty of majesty to attract us to him. Nothing in

94

his appearance that we should desire him. He was despised and rejected by men, a man of sorrows, and familiar with suffering. Like one from whom men hide their faces he was despised, and we esteemed him not. Surely he took up our infirmities and carried our sorrows, yet we consider him stricken by God, smitten by him, and afflicted. But he was pierced for our transgressions; he was crushed for our iniquities; the punishment that brought us peace was upon him, and by his wounds we are healed" (Isaiah 53:1-5, *International Version*).

Ethics for every day is Christological theology. The local church identifies with the living Christ in the situations where healing and reconciliation are needed. Those places are the family, the local congregation, the community of friends, the community of work and the community of wider relationships.

The local congregation must prepare persons for living in the family and the many communities of personal interactions. Hence, the local congregation must be more than a preaching station or a group of spectators who assemble for religious entertainment. The local church must be the home base for everyday ethics. It must be a laboratory, a classroom, a practice field, an ethical and moral gymnasium; a place where disciples can be trained, cultivated, and encouraged in disciplined Christian living. Such training is painful. It must take place in small groups. It must allow persons to grow at their own rate. The local church must work at becoming more open and loving and more giving and forgiving. Only when the local church becomes the home base for ethics will it gain credibility in a skeptical world. An unattractive congregation controlled by apathy and selfishness and dominated by dissension and disagreement will be unwelcome in healing the hurts of a wounded world. In *Unchanging Mission*, Douglas Webster defines mission in clear, crisp words: "Mission like ministry is the reverse of status seeking; it always involves the surrender of status."[6] The Apostle Paul drives home this idea in his Letter to the Philippians: "But whatever gain I had, I counted as loss for the sake of Christ" (Philippians 3:7, *Revised Standard Version*). A practical way of saying this is:

1. The local church is where the meaning of Christian discipleship is taught;
2. The local church is the gathered community of baptized believers in Jesus Christ who meet to reflect and celebrate through meaningful worship the work of God in the world;
3. The local church is where obedience to the demands of Jesus are taught;
4. The local church is an extended family where persons in a depersonalized world find support and encouragement for the living of these difficult days;
5. The local church is where imperfect people in response to God's grace and forgiveness, plan and prepare to execute the ministry of reconciling action in God's world;
6. The local church is where persons not only receive comfort but are also challenged to become suffering servants of righteousness in a sinful work, and
7. The local church is the home base where love for the world begins as the members learn not to condemn the world but to remember that "Love stoops to conquer; love gives to live; love dies to save."

I believe in Jesus Christ who was right when He, like each of us, just another individual who couldn't beat city hall, worked to change the status quo and was destroyed. Looking at Him I see how our intelligence is crippled, our imagination stifled, our efforts wasted because we do not live as He did. Every day I am afraid He died in vain because He is buried in our churches, because we have betrayed his revolution in our obedience to authority and our fear of it. I believe in Jesus Christ who rises again and again in our lives so that we will be free from prejudice and arrogance, from fear and hate, and will carry on his revolution and make way for his kingdom.

This continuing struggle that seeks the beautiful melody of the blending of love, justice, and power is rooted in hope. This hope is grounded in the universal God that motivated

Amos, the Eighth Century prophet to cry out: "But let judgment run down as waters, and righteousness as a mighty stream." This hope, grounded in "The universal I AM of history," motivated Jesus of Nazareth to travel to a rugged hill outside of Jerusalem to do His work of reconciling a world lost in alienation. From that cross, He cried out for reconciliation, "Father, forgive them; for they know not what they do."

This Christ of history and of personal experience moved Dr. King to die in hope:

"I may not get there with you but I want you to know tonight that we as a people will get to the promised land."

Let us continue in the struggle for justice with this living hope, "*Continua en la lucha.*"

FOOTNOTES:

[1]Allan Aubrey Boesak, *Farewell to Innocence*, New York, Orbis Books, Maryknoll, 1977, p. 1.

[2]Ibid., p. 11.

[3]Op. Cit. p. 11.

[4]Hugo Assman, *Theology for a National Church*, Maryknoll, New York, 1976, p. 129.

[5]Allan Aubrey Boesak, Ibid., p. 13.

[6]Douglas Webster, *Unchanging Mission*, Philadelphia, Fortress Press, 1955, p. 1.

The Continuing Struggle

An address presented to the Medical School
of the University of California at San
Francisco in a memorial to Dr. Martin Luther King, Jr.

"I may not get there with you, but I want you to know
that we as a people will get to the promised land."

With an ugly cloud of premonition of his own death, Dr.
Martin Luther King, Jr., the evening before his untimely end
in April, 1968, gave us those powerful and promising words
of hope. In an era of uncertainty the flickering flame of hope
needs constant care so that bright promise will not become
gray ashes of failure. The struggle continues.

The struggle to preserve human life in an environment of
decency and dignity is both a local, national, and international one. It is a struggle that is both personal and social. Dr.
King, a Nobel Prize winner, bore the tenuous torch of hope to
his crucifixion, and you and I have been reminded how fragile
this flame of hope is by Aleksandr Solzhenitsyn in his Nobel
Prize acceptance speech. In that message, he states: "Violence, less and less embarrassed by the limits imposed by
centuries of lawfulness, is brazenly and victoriously striding
across the whole world."[1]

Dom Helder Camara, the Roman Catholic Archbishop of

Recife, Brazil, has offered us a definition of violence number one. He says that it is a "violation of personhood."[2] This could take the form in institutional violence. Sometimes an institution destroys human dignity and individual self-worth. An institution in the name of progress and managerial technological know how can depersonalize and "thingify" persons by manipulating them as objects. Sometimes, in the name of science and research, institutions practice covert violence in relationships with employees and with persons who come to be served by the institutions.

I have seen institutions perpetuate covert violence within the laws of the judicial system. Institutions do not kill with knives; they draw no blood, nor do they break any bones, but they are often skillful in breaking the human spirit. They create feelings of self-worthlessness by continuing in age-old traditions that open doors for the favored, and by excluding genius among the latecomers who often find the door to equal opportunity closing as they approach it. Subtle manifestations of racism dressed in the gowns of academia, and couched in the elegant language of scholarship pose often as Mr. Benign Neglect or Mrs. Not Aware of Any Problem Existing. These manifestations of racism are far more sophisticated in public demeanor than the crude tactics of the American Nazi Party or the crass behavior of the Neo-Ku Klux Klan. The institutions of society can make systemic changes in their structures so that well-meaning persons would not be forced to work as perpetrators or victims of injustice.

Dr. Martin Luther King, Jr., was very fond of quoting St. Thomas Aquinas who said, "Unjust laws are acts of violence rather than laws." In "Summa Theologica," Aquinas stated: "If a law is not derived from the eternal law, and so lacking the true nature of law, it is rather a kind of violence."[3] Even Archie Bunker personality types are learning that Dr. Martin Luther King, Jr., was a universalist who spoke not only for the rights of black people, but of justice as a value for blue-collar white garbage workers in Mississippi, the oppressed of Vietnam, and the middle American whose economic rewards fall far below the hours and energy given on the job.

FOR THE FACING OF THIS HOUR

In *Worlds of Pain*, Lillian Breslow Rubin wrote:

"These are the people who had believed in the promise
of America, who had believed that if they deferred today's pleasures, they would reap tomorrow's rewards.
They had played by the rules of the game—rules that
promised anyone could make it if they tried hard
enough, worked hard enough. So they tried hard,
worked hard, obeyed the law, and taught their children
to do the same. In return, the lucky ones got a collection
of goods, a car, a house filled with expensive appliances,
perhaps a camper, a truck, or a boat. But the good life
eluded them; the game was rigged. The goods—not yet
paid for—often brought as many burdens as pleasures.
Life was hard."[4]

Racist politicians and some scholars in prestigious universities taught the blue-collar white worker and the middle-
class white professional that the blacks and other minorities
are the causes for the collapse of our materialistic, imper-
sonalized existence. Nothing was said about massive spending of tax money for military matter, nothing was told about
the tax breaks, oil-depletion allowances, price supports,
government-backed loans and government bail out of automobile corporations and railroads in the business sector.
While the poor struggle to exist on unemployment, under
employment, degradingly small subsistence payments, and
food stamps sold them by persons who despise the poor they
are paid to serve, and while inadequate medical and dental
care are the fare of the poor, investment continues within the
military industrial complex.

Respected American institutions support a president who
talks of human rights around the world while remaining mute
when this government and American universities and banks
join American corporations in investing and subsidizing a racist regime in South Africa. In American northern, eastern,
and western urban areas, the practice of the doctrine of benign
neglect has sent many professionally trained blacks back to
southern urban areas where white professionals with a south-

ern accent do a far greater job of accepting blacks within the letter of the law and the spirit of love than many "so-called liberal Yankees." In fact, infant mortality in East Oakland and East Palo Alto is among the highest in the nation.

The struggle continues at home. Many gains made during the decade of the sixties have eroded. The seventies undid much of what Dr. King and his supporters accomplished for liberation. The decade of the eighties does not give an easy promise for the changing of this ugly nightmare of violence and hatred into a realized dream of brotherhood. Hence, the struggle continues.

The struggle is against bigotry and is for brotherhood. The struggle is against the present practice of pitting woman against men, and men against women. The struggle is against 20 percent of the people of the world controlling 80 percent of the world's resources. The struggle is calling for a coalition of persons who will continue in the struggle against racism, sexism, neo-colonialism, and all other isms that create and perpetuate schisms in the human family. This struggle seeks to balance in perfect harmony the triad of love, justice, and power. Power without love is exploitation. Love without power is the paralysis of good will. Love without justice is weak and paternalistic sentimentality cut off from any ethical roots. Justice without love loses the balance between retribution and redemption and is heartless and inhumane.

The struggle continues because we still have too few minorities entering the expensive and exclusive medical profession. Even brilliant students find that they must arm themselves against the evils of subtle racism within the institutions of learning while continuing the never-ending battle with banks to lend them money for tuition costs. When young black doctors begin their practices, insurance companies, Medi-Cal, and other medical plans red line them for practicing in ghetto communities by paying lower fees than those for comparable services in more affluent neighborhoods. Hospitals are not always open to younger minority physicians and even veteran doctors complain about the closed and clannish manner in which white physicians exclude them from opportunities to get referrals in the areas of their speciality.

Among the elderly poor are white persons who suffer with minorities for the lack of comprehensive medical services. Doctors who give treatment to the elderly wait far too long for their payments from state and federal programs of subsidy. Hence, some doctors refuse to treat poor, elderly or Medicare patients. These doctors should not have to wait an endless period of time for their money. Health alliances and community health clinics, such as the one made famous in East Oakland by Dr. Israel Dunn, are penalized by county, state and federal health bureaucrats because of their commitment to serve persons who are poor. Unnecessary guidelines and paper work that change from month to month and from funding period to funding period discourage serious health care professionals who want to help humankind. Hence, the struggle continues.

The struggle against violence that denigrates persons' sense of self-worth due to their inequality in receiving adequate education, health, cultural enrichment and economic opportunity persists in every society. Martin Luther King, Jr., if he is taken more seriously in death than he was in life, provides four ways for facing the continuing struggle:

1. Using existing institutions such as churches to challenge and change the system;
2. Using nonviolent tactics to dramatize evil in the system;
3. Developing new institutions such as Southern Christian Leadership Conference, People United to Save Humanity, and Opportunities Industrialization Centers, and to use these institutions to challenge the structure and replace time worn, ineffective social change organizations that have become ineffective, and
4. Direct action in struggle and suffering to produce the change that comes about only by total commitment.

If the struggle for justice continues, churches must recruit young persons and train them for a prophetic ministry in God's world. Young professional persons must be trained to not be so much a part of the system that they cannot see the evils of the system. As persons of talent and training, they must be challenged to work with sophistication against subtle manifestations of evil in their own professions and to see covert examples of racism at their places of work. Just as saints of God were an underground movement in Ahab's palace, so today must our professionally trained young people work as moral and ethical change agents, quietly, covertly, patiently and wisely, suffering long for the truth of God to become incarnate in the marketplaces of this world of cultural pluralism.

So-called Christians in the white community appeal to their own ignorance of the evils in the system. They are unaware of past and present inequities. They are blind to racist practices in controlling the advancement and progress of minorities. They are unaware of a racism that limits the numbers of blacks who will hold political offices in America, will exclude blacks from board membership in the corporate structure, and will assign blacks primarily to community service or public relations positions in the major corporations of America. They are innocent because they are not aware of a racism in sports that excludes black stars from coaching positions in the American football league. Upon retirement many famous black football stars become anonymous and discarded objects left to live without the T.V. commercial spots or radio-television announcing jobs given to other retiring athletes. Many black athletes are conversant and eloquent in the use of middle-class standard English and their academic training well fits them for many job opportunities now denied them.

This continuing struggle in the black ghetto against absentee landlords who allow their property to decay and deflate in price, and white persons who enter the ghetto by paying top dollars for the property and after pouring in thousands of dollars to improve the property they move into the community which is now far too expensive taxwise and otherwise for the original dwellers to remain. This process of gentrification is a challenge to Christianity.

The tragedy of white theological education is that white clergy can study Hebrew, Greek, Bible, philosophy, theology, church history, pastoral care, and administration, and upon graduating from divinity school remain aloof, alienated, and angry toward the struggle that continues. The struggle against ignorance and blindness in places where light and wisdom ought to prevail is one which the church cannot escape. The trouble with black clergy is that they are either carbon copies of the schools that trained them, or their own ego needs to promote themselves as leading orators on the preaching circuit blinds them to God's call to face the challenge of his hour with the same prophetic commitment of Martin Luther King, Jr., who died in hope, saying, "I may not get there with you, but I want you to know that we as a people will get to the promised land." The eschatology of Dr. Martin Luther King, Jr. is rooted in biblical and theological ethics as a result of his American experience and American education, yet prestigious American theologians travel to Germany in pursuit of a relevant and authentic theology of hope.

FOOTNOTES:

[1]Robert McAfee Brown, *Religion and Violence*, Philadelphia, Westminister Press, 1973, p. 29.

[2]Ibid., p. 9.

[3]Op. cit., p. 9.

[4]Lillian Breslow Rubin, *Worlds of Pain*, Life in the Working Class Family, New York, Basic Books, Inc., Publisher, 1974, pp.5-6.

The Black Church and the Facing of This Hour

"The spirit of the Lord is upon me because he has anointed me; He has sent me to announce good news to the poor, to proclaim release for prisoners and recovery of sight for the blind; to let the broken victims go free, to proclaim the year of the Lord's favor" (Luke 4:18-19, *New English Bible*).

Liberation was the theme of the deeds of Jesus in the world. His ministry was in the streets. Persons who were excluded from the established classes of society were the objects of His love and service. He gave comfort to the despised and the disinherited. The demon-possessed, ostracized by society, were given sanity and acceptance. The sick, lame, blind and maimed were loved and not blamed for their pitiful plight.

If the church is to be the living presence of Jesus Christ in the world, the deeds of ministry must touch not only the respected classes who wear the name Christian, but persons alienated from Christ and His church must be touched with the love of Jesus. The church cannot forget the many young persons in prison, out of school, unemployed, or stigmatized by a jail record. Too often the church is locked into beautiful stained-glass window sanctuaries with cushioned seats, crimson carpets and air-conditioned comfort. A liberating Christ invites the church to move into a world of alienation, hostility, hopelessness, failure and death for the purpose of bringing healing and good news.

FOR THE FACING OF THIS HOUR

Lepers, demoniacs, prostitutes, pimps, arrogant and smug middle-class Pharisees, puffed with pride over mythological success in a false economy, are in dire need of liberation. Self-righteous Christians whose sinful pride blinds them to their involvement in perpetrating unjust economic, educational and political structures need their eyes opened to the truth about themselves so that the darkness of self-delusion will not forever hold them in a prison of oppression. Those immoral majority Christians masquerading under an apron of culturally conditioned fig leaves as exponents of the moral majority need to know that, as modern Jews they are as sinful as modern secular oriented Gentiles. "For all have sinned, and come short of the glory of God" (Romans 3:23). But liberation in Christ frees church members from self-righteous pride as well as Gentile, secular persons whose sensate life-style worships their appetites and the gods of creation, rather than the Creator.

Jesus, the liberator, was fully God and fully man. He was in our lowliness what He is in His majesty. As man He did not worship creation and its creatures, but He was able to relate us properly to God through obedience, lowliness, and humiliation. Jesus knew the limitations of the flesh which produced in Himself hunger, thirst, fatigue and the need for human companionship and assistance from His disciples and from persons like Mary and Martha. Although He was God in the sense of Johannine Christology, He was also man. Therefore, Jesus helped us to reconcile ourselves beyond our humanity, as did Adam, so as to seek equality with God. This liberation act should enable clergy to accept human limitations and the need for a team ministry with lay persons. Clergy persons are not superpersons. Clergy need to be ministered unto by the very lay persons to whom they minister. Hence, clergy and laity have a symbiotic relationship of mutual support and interdependence. In the author's ministry, this reality of the priesthood of the believers, as taught by Martin Luther and John Calvin, is illustrated with the following unsolicited letters which come from lay members:

FOR THE FACING OF THIS HOUR

Letter dated July 31, 1981 from Mrs. Sharon Banks titled *On Encouragement.*

Dear Pastor Smith:

It does not seem as though five years have passed since February, 1976 when I first learned that Mother had terminal lung cancer.

I clearly remember your encouraging visit to our home and the Scripture you read and reminded me of—2 Corinthians 4. It is as comforting now as it was on that day.

When mother died that July 31, I felt an ache inside for months but was comforted and encouraged by God's word, the True Comforter, family, and friends. The encouragement I received sustained me and made me know that "We are troubled on every side, yet not distressed; we are perplexed, but not in despair." (2 Corinthians 4:8)

Today is the fifth anniversary of Mother's homegoing. Yesterday, I completed the California Bar examination. Five years ago I was overwhelmed with grief and loss. I realize now I was "cast down but not destroyed," thanks to God's grace and love. Encouragement has been the key avenue through which God has assured me during this experience. I was reminded of encouragement in your Pastor's Pen of August 3, 1981. Encouragement is something that has to come from others—spouse, family, friends, even strangers. It is all but impossible for us to encourage *ourselves* in the same way that others can encourage us.

My testimony is that Jesus did indeed send a Comforter. I don't exactly know when that ache in me subsided, but it has.

Upon this reflection I write you today, Pastor Smith, to encourage you in all the challenges you face as person and pastor of Allen Temple. Thank you for your encouragement and continued prayers for us. The God who we serve *is* our Rock.

"I will love thee, O Lord, my strength. The Lord is my rock, and my fortress, and my deliverer; My

God, my strength, in whom I will trust; my buckler, and the horn of my salvation, and my high tower. I will call upon the Lord, who is worthy to be praised; so shall I be saved from mine enemies" (Psalms 18:1-3).

In His Love,
Sharon Banks/s/

Letter dated July 29, 1981 from Mr. and Mrs. H. Vincent Price:

Dear Pastor Smith:

This letter is written out of deep love, respect and concern for a worldly man under the guidance of our heavenly Father. This man, Pastor Smith, is you.

Weekly we receive the church Bulletin and we are overwhelmed at how heavy your schedule is. We cannot express in words our deepest and most sincere concern for your well-being. You visit the sick, shut-in, the hospitalized, the weary, are a writer of endless articles, lectures, sermons, etc., teach Bible study, meet with the Ministers in Training, are a marriage counselor, are an outspoken representative on the Oakland Public School Board, not to mention the construction site. These are just some of your countless responsibilities.

You have done so much for all *people*, especially the *people* in East Oakland. Those who come in contact with you or know of you, cannot help but feel your strength, love, discipline and self-assurance. However, Pastor Smith, you are one man. We know that you wish to help solve or attempt to help solve everyone's problems, etc., but you are but one of our Almighty Lord's soldiers.

Pastor Smith, do take time to rest. If at any time we may be of service, please do not hesitate to contact us directly or through our parents.

Give Mrs. Smith and the rest of your lovely family our deepest love and respect.

The Black Church and the Facing of This Hour

With sincere love, respect and pride for our pastor and friend,

Mr. and Mrs. H. Vincent Price/s/

Jesus Christ, the liberator, comes to us with good news as neighbor. The gospel of liberation calls the church to be contemporaneous with Jesus, the liberator. This means that church members cannot escape into irrelevant Bible study that concerns itself with safe issues, such as debates over eschatology and Scriptural interpretations that are abstract, but the church must face contemporary Calvaries where persons die on crosses of poverty, drug addiction, racism, ecological sin and exploitation.

Liberation in Christ means that the church must be a participant in the grace of God so that Christians take on themselves vicariously the sins of others in order to create unity and peace with God, nature and humankind through the ministry of reconciliation. This action calls for sacrifice, suffering and service by walking by faith where the church cannot see, and by appropriating into the motives of the church the mind of Jesus Christ. Liberation Christology has its roots in Pauline Christology as expressed in Galatians 2:19-20: "For I through the law as died to the law, that I might live unto God. I am crucified with Christ: nevertheless I live; yet not I, but Christ liveth in me; and the life which I now live in the flesh I live by the faith of the Son of God, who loved me, and gave himself for me."

Liberation Christology may lead the church to crucifixion, but God will raise the church from death unto life, just as He raised Jesus from the dead and gave Him a name which is above every name.

Jesus as liberator frees this sinful world from the penalty, presence and power of sin. The freedom from the penalty of sin is regeneration and is in past tense. The freedom from the presence of sin is sanctification and is in present tense. The freedom from the power of sin is glorification and is in the future tense. Christians have been saved, are being saved, and will be saved. Jesus as liberator saves the church from allegiance to dead traditions, from the refusal to change to meeting new challenges, and from the biases of culture and color. Hence, if in Christ all persons are equal, racial, sexual, class, and cultural distinctions have no place in the church. Yet racism divides the church of today and women have a second-class status in ministry. Educated clergy sometimes exclude from the craft more creative and gifted non-seminary trained persons whose charisma far outshines the academic sterility of some so-called professional ministers. On the other side of the coin, too many clergy who were too lazy to endure the rigors of academic preparation, allow envy and jealousy to create non-Christian attitudes toward clergy who love God with their intellectual, emotional and volitional selves. "For through faith you are all sons of God in union with Christ Jesus. Baptized into union with him, you have all put on Christ as a garment. There is no such thing as Jew and Greek, slave and freeman, male and female; for you are all one person in Christ Jesus" (Galatians 3:26-29, *New English Bible*).

Liberation in Christ demands that the church proclaim the Gospel of the kingdom of God. This means that the church must never echo the creed of her culture but must cry out with a trumpet the justice-oriented message of the rule of God which allows injustice to be the ruling ethic. Many so-called liberal white denominations have large investments in hundreds of American firms which are reaping profit from the disgraceful economics of the Union of South Africa. In addition to this, many white churches own thousands of acres in the south where black sharecroppers are being pushed off the land into already crowded ghettos. White churches spend thousands of dollars on contracts for building programs from businesses and contractors that practice racial discrimination in hiring.

Black churches in America are part of an economic and political system that oppresses black, brown and yellow persons of the third world. Eighty percent of the world's resources are at the disposal of only about 20 percent of the world population, most of whom are white and live in the

North Atlantic region. These 20 percent control 90 percent of the world's income, 90 percent of the gold reserves, 95 percent of its scientific knowledge, 70 percent of its meat and 80 percent of its protein. Because of the vested interests and historical involvement of white theologians and churches in oppression, very few prophetic efforts will emerge from white seminaries and denominational leaders. The racism of white seminaries is so blinding to white intellectuals that they will omit black theology as an academic discipline, while demanding that minority and majority students master English theology, German theology, Continental theology, Japanese theology, American theology and process theology. Black persons who study at white schools must liberate themselves from Anglo-Saxon cultural blindness so as to be fit for a prophetic black ministry among the last, least and lowest. Jesus, the liberator, identifies with those who are despised and rejected of men. Liberation theology in the black tradition proclaims Jesus as a man of sorrows, acquainted with grief. Black spirituals carry the theological content of hope and liberation. Black spirituals believe in a religion of the reversals of conditions of the rich and the poor, the proud and the meek, of master and slave. The Jesus of the oppressed enabled black Christian slaves to project into the future what the present denied them. Jesus, the liberator, was for them good news and the bringer of good news. Liberation in Christ helps persons to live a credible life in an incredible world. If the white church would repent of arrogance and pride, and if the black church would repent of the sin of irresponsibility and scapegoating, black and white Christians could experience liberation in Christ, and a new and authentic reconciliation would open the graves in which society is entombed, so that a new humanity or a new creation in Christ will not only be a possibility, but will also compose the opening chapters of a new genesis for human kind.

"Yes, I am coming soon, and bringing my recompense with me, to requite everyone according to his deeds. I am the Alpha and the Omega, the first and the last, the beginning and the end.

He who gives this testimony speaks: Yes, I am coming soon. Amen. Come, Lord Jesus. The grace of the Lord be with you all" (Revelation 22: 12-13, 20-21, *New English Bible*).

God's Power, God's Church, and the New Reconstruction

An address to the Twenty-Third Annual
Session of Progressive Baptist State
Convention of California and Nevada,
July 16, 1981, Bethany Baptist Church,
Oakland, California.

Introduction

Overeating produces an unpleasant feeling. When we over-eat, we feel guilty because our eyes were larger than our stomachs, and because we gorged ourselves, while millions suffer and die from malnutrition. Overeating and obesity are among the chief sins of pagan and Christian America. Woe be unto us in the day of God's judgment!

You and I can also overeat mentally so that we feel the piercing pain of intellectual indigestion. However, far too few of us suffer on this wise. Too many of us suffer from mental malnutrition. We ignore educational television, reject membership in a monthly book club, and find no intellectual content in our Christian expressions. At the same time, we deplore messages from the pulpit that have sense emphasized more than the sweet sounds of "whoopolistic artistry." Black Baptists have never been guilty of overeating in their studies of the Bible and Christian education. Black Baptists tend to pick up their faith primarily through a feeling of osmosis, rather than through a process that obeys II Timothy 2:15

which says: "Study to shew thyself approved unto God, a workman that needeth not to be ashamed, rightly dividing the word of truth."

Perhaps our undereating of the Bible and theology is why the program committee gave me such a long theme to speak on. This theme, if taken seriously, can produce mental indigestion. It is far too lengthy and has far too many scriptures for adequate discussion in a thirty-minute time context. Nevertheless, I shall touch briefly on God's power, God's church, and the new reconstruction as it relates to black and brown Americans in the decade of the nineteen eighties. I am impressed with that part of the theme which calls for the new reconstruction. This suggests an old reconstruction. What was the old reconstruction for the black community?

The Black Reconstruction (1867-1876)

From 1867 to 1876 black Americans enjoyed their greatest tokens of freedom after the emancipation of 1863. Tokens of freedom and trappings of power, trimmings of democracy and scraps of human rights describe reconstruction. Many white historians deny my thesis that the reconstruction period was one of tokenism. They argue against the period as one of black irresponsibility and the exploitation of the white south by northern carpetbaggers. Dr. W. E. B. DuBois pointed to the accomplishments of reconstruction governments. He called attention to the new democratic constitutions, to the beginnings of a public-school system, to the reconstruction of war-ravaged public facilities and to various social reforms. He reminded his colleagues of all that Negroes had done to help themselves, their churches, schools, and colleges, and self-help projects. He placed the corruption and malfeasance of reconstruction in the larger light of American history, arguing that it was not restricted to carpetbaggers and Negroes. He supported the character and quality of many of the important Negro officeholders. Finally, DuBois remained unrepentant about reconstruction. He concluded with bitter irony: "Practically the whole new growth of the south has been accomplished under laws which black men helped to frame

114

thirty years ago. I know of no greater compliment to Negro suffrage."[1]

The first reconstruction was a period of black advance: black churches and denominations came into being; black schools and colleges were born; black ministers moved from the pulpit in the church building to a pulpit in public places, thus identifying with Amos, Hosea, Micah, Jesus and Paul. Progress did not come easily.

Defeated white southerners resented the loss of their slave property. They were angry because their farm or agrarian economy had been ravaged. Northern labor unions closed their doors to black members who were skilled artisans. Dr. Wyatt T. Walker said that those who could not find work in the industrial north were forced to return to the south to work as sharecroppers and that "sharecropping became the legitimate first cousin to slavery."[2] Dr. William A. Jones, lecturing at Colgate Rochester/Berkeley Hall/Crozer Theological Seminary in Rochester, New York, said: "Lincoln didn't free the slaves. He fired them."[3]

In the north, blacks shut out of membership in the unions were given the ugly name of strikebreakers when they went to work. In 1869 they organized the National Negro Labor Union, which met with little success, since it did not have the support of white labor officials. In the south, blacks who were sharecroppers went into economic slavery because the landowners who sold the sharecroppers the lease were also the local storekeepers who sold food and supplies on credit until the crop could be harvested. This practice of stealing with high interest rates left black people in permanent economic slavery.

In the south, secret societies such as the Knights of the White Camelia, the White Brotherhood, and the Ku Klux Klan used terror, lynchings, and lawlessness to regain power and to prevent blacks from enjoying the Fourteenth and Fifteenth Amendments of citizenship and voting rights for blacks.

On March 4, 1877 the period of reconstruction ended and black power was buried with the election of Republican Rutherford B. Hayes to the Presidency of the United States.

The southern states had all federal troops withdrawn. Blacks had no one but Jesus to protect them from the ravages of racism.

The Need for a New Reconstruction

The old reconstruction reminds us of the need for a new reconstruction. Programs funded by the federal government which have helped to alleviate black suffering and to eliminate black injustice are being defunded by Congress and President Ronald Reagan. Yet, the problems persist.

In *Portrait of Inequality: Black and White Children in America*, Dr. Edelman said:

"A black baby is twice as likely to die the first year of his life as is a white.

Black teenagers die of heart and congenital defects at twice the rate of white teenagers.

They are twice as likely as white children to have no regular source of health care.

A black baby is twice as apt to be born and locked into poverty throughout his childhood.

His mother goes out earlier to work, works longer hours and is paid less. He is twice as apt to live with neither parent and to grow up in a family whose head has not finished high school. As a teenager he is twice as likely to be arrested for serious property crimes and again twice as likely to be detained in a juvenile or adult correctional facility. If both his parents work, they earn but half what an equivalent white couple earns. He is twice as likely to drop out of school, twice as apt to lag in grade level, half as apt to be termed gifted, and three times as likely to be labeled educable mentally retarded. His path is an uphill struggle against the odds and the longer he stays in school, the more he lags. If he graduates from high school his chance for employment is less than that of a white who drops out of elementary school; the odds for his employment if he is a college graduate is equal to those of a white high school drop out."[4]

According to Dr. Nathan Wright, between 40 and 50 percent or nearly one-half of all of our black youth are functional illiterates. This means that they cannot read above the fourth-grade level. Churches must be heartsick to know that a generation is on the scene that cannot intelligently read the Scriptures.

The need for a new reconstruction is ever before us. Churches cannot carry on business as usual. While the very future of our children and grandchildren hangs in balance, our church members relish pettiness and not prayer, gossip and not the good news, moral laxity and not spiritual vitality. While racism seeks to disrespect our heritage, damage our present and destroy our future, we diminish our mission to songs, prayers and sermons, rejecting the crisis of a world waiting for rescue, regeneration, redemption and reconstruction. Have we not heard, have we not understood, have we not acted upon the revelation that:

"God was in Christ, reconciling the world unto himself, not imputing their trespasses unto them; and hath committed unto us the word of reconciliation" (II Cor. 5:19).

God has a new reconstruction. Not the atheistic socialism of Marx, not the greedy capitalism of American multinational corporations, not the barren intellectualism of the university, or the fruitless, futile theories of political science, but God has a new reconstruction.

God has a plan of new reconstruction. God has a solution for a world waiting for rescue, regeneration, redemption and reconstruction. God has a system for bringing out of the chaos of current culture, a newly reconstructed culture of common good.

God's power in His church, God's power of His church, God's power for His church and God's power through His church will help to actualize the new reconstruction.

> "Now unto him that is able to do exceeding abundantly above all that we ask or think, according to the power that worketh in us" (Ephesians 3:20).

God's Formula for the New Reconstruction

God has a plan for realizing the new reconstruction. His plan is to use His power and us. We are not puny, powerless pygmies. We are those through whom God works. Through us God's power labors. Through us God's power lifts. Through us God's power loves.

> The reconciling word,
> The refreshing word,
> The renewing word,
> The regenerating word,
> The redeeming word,
>> shared with us,
>> given to us,
>> entrusted to us,
>> treasured by us,
>
> *destructs, constructs, and reconstructs when we share this living word with God's power.*

As Hans Kung has said, "The gospel has no blueprint for dealing with specific solutions for the knotty problems of nuclear waste, over-population, and energy and pollution problems."[5] However the Gospel of peace that we preach does testify that God rescues, regenerates, redeems and reconstructs human hearts. Unselfish persons, loving persons, sacrificing persons are the creation of God's new reconstruction. No degrees in the humanities can make persons less greedy. No degrees in the social sciences or in psychology can make society less egocentric. Only God's power at work within us can transform our conduct above the conformity of the deformed. Our elders called this experience conversion.

Theologians call it a divine-human encounter.

The Conclusion
1. Such an encounter is the cause for celebration and praise in worship.
2. I imagine Jacob celebrated when his name was changed to Israel.
3. I imagine Zaccheus celebrated when Jesus changed his life.
4. I imagine Paul celebrated after his Damascus road experience.
5. I am sure John on the Isle of Patmos celebrated in the Spirit on the Lord's Day, after having a vision of this old age passing away, while a new age was being born.

This too is for ultimate hope. We await the coming of the New Reconstruction in its fullness. Our prayers yearn for that day. Like John we utter, "Even so, come, Lord Jesus."

FOOTNOTES:

[1]Drimmer, Melvin, editors, *Black History, a Reappraisal:* Garden City, New York, Anchor Books, Doubleday & Co., Inc., 1969, p. 272.

[2]Walker, Wyatt T., *Somebody's Calling My Name*, Valley Forge, Judson Press, 1979, p. 81.

[3]Op. Cit., p. 81.

[4]*The Crisis, A Record of the Darker Races*, May, 1981, Vol. 88, No. 4, Whole Number 781, Book Corner, p. 205.

[5]Küng, Hans; *On Being a Christian*, New York City, Doubleday & Co., 1976, pg. 596.

Our Theological Task

Theologians today approach their tasks with a holistic world view that refuses to divorce hell from housing, regeneration from racism, justification from justice, prayer from pollution, salvation from starvation, or worship from work.

German theologian Helmut Gollwitzer sets the pace in declaring: "Every article of the confession of faith has explosive and aggressive significance for the status quo of the old world, an article that leaves our relationship to the other man and to society as it was, is not worthy to be an article of the Christian faith."[1]

I believe that those negative carpers of criticism who deprecate the diligent digging of theological realities in the disciplined context of the seminary environment are forgetting the first law of the theological experience. That law, if it is permissible to transpose Etienne Gilson's remarks, is "theology always buries its undertakers."[2]

Some of the popular disenchantment with theology can be laid at the door of the death-of-God theologians who failed to use a clear language in which to present their ideas. What they argued was that a God conceived in independence from the world of human consciousness and ruling over His creation was a concept to be discarded. This was a reaction against the transcendent God of Karl Barth. *Death of God Thinker*, by Thomas Altizer, taught that we needed to rediscover Hegel's vision of "a God who revealed Himself through the secular experience of the process of change in human history."[3]

FOR THE FACING OF THIS HOUR

Following the failure of the theology of the death of God, came the theologians of hope. One cannot help but notice that Professor Jurgen Moltmann in his *Theology of Hope* introduces his closing remarks by quoting Hegel's dialectical theory, "A thing is alive only when it contains contradiction within itself and is indeed the power of holding the contradiction within itself and enduring it."[4]

It is this human capability that gives purpose, meaning, and freedom to our lives as well as the capacity for handling creatively "events and processes" which are open toward the future of God. This locus of theological thrust points us to hope in the not-yet of the future of God as the basis or foundation of our present believing.

It protects us from the theological humanism of Rabbi Richard Rubenstein who, in his book, *After Auschwitz*, preached that the Biblical concept of a just God who is the omnipotent judge of the world must be rejected because Jews cannot harmonize the justice of God with Auschwitz. Secularists would agree with Rubenstein, and call the courting of a Calvinistic doctrine of God's sovereignity a theological obscenity, while others would call it a Jewish theodicy.

Black theologian Joseph Washington refutes the position of Rubenstein and makes a fresh contribution to American theological dialogue in his major work, *The Politics of God.* Washington affirms that blacks may have been chosen to play the suffering-servant role in society as the present-day chosen people of God. Washington sees black suffering pregnant with redemptive possibilities. He states: "The universal task God assigned to the Jews was to inform the human family that there is one and only one God. The universal mission of blacks is parallel: to witness to the one humanity of the one God."[5] Respected theologian J. Deotis Roberts follows Washington in supporting the Biblical model of the suffering servant for blacks in observing: "The resurrection is the sequel to the cross. Without Easter morning, Good Friday would be Bad Friday for evil would have the last word."[6] A younger black thinker at Union Theological Seminary named James Cone maintains that God has not chosen blacks for

121

redemptive suffering, but for freedom, because their suffering is not voluntary but involuntary, which is the antithesis of the suffering role of Jesus Christ.[7]

Martin Luther King, Jr., was a Ph.D. in theology and was qualified to speak as both a peerless preacher and a penetrating thinker in theology. Dr. King did not pit the oppressor and the oppressed against each other, but his understanding of God's love and forgiveness called for a redemption of friend and foe into a newer community of two alien groups becoming one in Jesus Christ. This was no wild-eyed utopian delusion but a creative possibility for those who believe in the God who makes all things new. Finally, the challenge comes to lay and professional theologians alike from Gustavo Gutierrez, who says: "Instead of using only revelation and tradition as starting points, as classical theology has generally done, it must start with facts and questions derived from the world and from history."[8] Though you may have second thoughts about Gutierrez's assumption, remember that in the pastoral context, the persons in the pews come to the pastor-counselor with the hurts, doubts, fears and questions of their contextual situations. It is to these situations that they ask of you, "Is there any word from the Lord?" It is to these situations and to our own pathos and anguish that you seek the word from home that will bring wholeness.

This is our theological task. Let us perform this task hearing Jesus who is the Great Commission, the Man who is sent and who Himself is the message.[9] Let us remember, "He uttered a triumphant cry: "It is accomplished! And it was as though He had said: Everything has begun."[10]

At the American Baptist Seminary of the West we educate young women and men to proclaim in word and deed the message that "God was in Christ reconciling the world unto Himself." This message is taught by rigorous thinkers who love the church, especially the parish, with a passionate intensity.

The Biblical commitment, evangelical fervor, and pastoral heart, merged with ripe scholarship, come from the prolific pen of our theologian, Dr. Russell Aldwinckle, who writes: "It does not follow that the hope of heaven necessarily means that one is against earth, however one-sided some Christians have been in the past. In a truly Christian, and not a cynical sense, the case can be made that one of the glories of the Christian faith is that a man can have the best of both worlds. The present world with all its possibilities, is after all God's world. What comes after death is also in His hands. The Christian hope spans both time and eternity and we should not opt for less."[11] Under Dr. Aldwinckle and the other faculty members, ABSW students develop thoughtful, reasoned, and critical answers to those questions so prevalent in an age of doubt.

In *The Living God and the Modern World*, Cambridge scholar Peter Hamilton reminds us that in an age of doubt, our theological task is to "reaffirm the reality of God by showing Him to be actively at work within the natural order."[12] We, at ABSW are serious about our theological task. We agree with theologian A. Durwood Foster that "the vision of the Supremacy of Christ like love is still pregnant with creative implications for Western man as well as for the future of the whole world."[13]

ABSW communicates a word about the supremacy of Christ for the modern world. But beyond the practice of "intellectual ping pong," ABSW in classroom reflections that intersect theory with practice, promotes a theological task of "God in us . . . ensures the continuing presence of Jesus' word in a creative way."[14]

Yes, our theological task, as Dr. Abraham Heschel reminds us is to be "in travail with God's dreams and designs, with God's dream of a world redeemed, of reconciliation of heaven and earth, of a mankind which is truly His image, reflecting His wisdom, justice, and compassion."[15] Come, my friends, and join us in this quest.

Our Theological Task

FOOTNOTES:

[1]Helmut Gollwitzer, *The Rich Christians and Poor Lazarus*, New York, The MacMillan Co., 1970, p. 3.

[2]Etienne Gilson, *The Unity of Philosophical Experience*, New York: Charles Scribner's Sons, 1937, p. 306.

[3]Carl E. Armerding, editor, *Evangelicals and Liberation*, Nutley, New Jersey: Presbyterian and Reformed Publishing Co., 1977, p. 2.

[4]Ibid., p. 3.

[5]Joseph Washington, *The Politics of God*, Boston: Beacon Press, 1969, p. 158.

[6]J. Deotis Roberts, *Liberation and Reconciliation: A Black Theology*, Philadelphia: Westminster Press, 1971, pp. 83-172.

[7]James Cone, *A Black Theology of Liberation*, New York: Lippincott, 1970, p. 7.

[8]Gustavo Gutierrez, *A Theology of Liberation*, New York: Maryknoll, 1973, p. 7.

[9]Max Warren, *I Believe in the Great Commission*, Grand Rapids: Wm. B. Eerdmans Publishing Co., pp. 16-17.

[10]George Marsden, *Demythologizing Evangelicalism: A Review of Donald W. Dayton's Discovering an Evangelical Heritage*, Christian Scholars' Review, Volume VII, No. 2, 3, 1977, Houghton, New York.

[11]Russell Aldwinckle, *Death in the Secular City*, Grand Rapids, Michigan, William B. Eerdmans Publishing Co., 1972, p. 23.

[12]Peter Hamilton, *The Living God and the Modern World*, Philadelphia, Penn., United Church Press, 1967, p. 4.

[13]A. Durwood Foster, *The God Who Loves*, New York: Collier-MacMillan Limited, 1971, p. 5.

[14]Juan Luis Segundo, *Our Idea of God*, New York: Maryknoll.

[15]Abraham J. Heschel, *Who Is Man*, Stanford University Press, Stanford, California, 1965, p. 119.

A Christian Philosophy
for Facing This Hour

The fatalistic interpretation of life holds that fate or the gods determine the path for human beings. Persons cannot change history or shape the future. What will be will be. A classic example of this philosophy is found in Sophocles' tragedy, *Oedipus*. A son was born into the king's family. Prior to his birth the oracle stated that he would murder his father and marry his mother. The king sought to defeat this ugly decree by giving orders that the son would die by exposure on the mountainside. A tender-hearted servant, commanded to execute the king's desires, weakened and gave the child to pilgrims passing through the land. These travelers carried the baby into a far country where the child was eventually adopted as a prince of the royal household. When the prince became a young adult he learned of his fate as was told by the oracle. Thinking that his foster parents were his real parents and striving to escape from the dual evils of incest and patricide, he fled from the palace into a distant kingdom which was the land of his birth. There he met his true parents. In ignorance, he fell in love with his mother whom he found to be beautiful and took her to be his wife after killing his father, the king. It was only after a child was born to this incestuous relationship that he discovered that the prophecy which the oracle foretold had come to pass.

A Christian Philosophy for Facing This Hour

An unknown poet has written:

We are no other than a moving row of visionary shapes
that come and go round with this sun-illumined lantern
held in midnight by the master of the show.

This philosophy of fatalism taught that humans are puppets on the string of fate, villains by necessity, fools by
heavenly compulsion, knaves by spherical predominance,
and liars by forces and influences external to human subjec-
tivity.

Later on in history some thinkers taught that human nature
was totally depraved, due to inborn and inherited sin. Some
theologians said that God from all eternity, did by the most
wise and holy counsel of His own will, freely and unchange-
ably determine what would come to pass. Some persons and
angels are predestined unto everlasting life and others unto
everlasting death. From my class lectures in church history
comes to mind a story which was told to the class by our
erudite professor. An intensely Calvinistic preacher was used
to carrying his rifle to protect himself from unfriendly In-
dians. His wife asked him to leave the rifle at home since no
Indian could kill him until his time had come. He defended
his non-Calvinistic argument by telling his wife that he was
carrying the gun because he might meet an Indian whose time
had come.

In addition to fatalism and Calvinism, many scientific
minds are preaching a mechanistic philosophy which takes
us back to the days of Democritus, who lived four hundred
years before Christ. Democritus taught that humanlike behavior of animals is purely mechanistic. But he did not apply
this rule to human conduct. Herbert Spencer explained
human behavior on the basis of compound reflexes. Many
young college students from our churches give up their faith
to accept a new faith in a stimulus-response formula after
experimenting with guinea pigs, rats, muscles and glands.

Those persons who believe in free will and human responsibility reject fatalism, Calvinism, mechanism and other

"isms" which interpret human behavior. An anonymous poet expresses the philosophy of personal responsibility for human behavior and for influencing history by writing:

One ship drives east and
Another west, while the
Self-same breezes blow:
It is the set of the sails,
Not of the gales, which
Bids them the way to go.

It is my personal view that all persons have God as the future. All persons can share in a future that radiates the glory and presence of God. Paul plants this idea in my mind in Ephesians 1:9-10:

God has given us the wisdom to understand fully the mystery, the plan he was pleased to decree in Christ, to be carried out in the fulness of time, namely, to bring all things in the heavens and on earth into one under Christ's headship.

No tragedy or failure can take away this future. Persons in need of hope and encouragement can proclaim with Paul:

"For I am persuaded, that neither death, nor life, nor principalities, nor powers, nor things present, nor things to come, Nor height, nor depth, nor any other creature, shall be able to separate us from the love of God, which is in Christ Jesus our Lord" (Romans 8:38-39).

When persons read history theologically, they see the interdependence of the doctrines of creation, covenant, incarnation, crucifixion, resurrection, and eschatology and the future of humankind makes sense. There is a thread of purpose and meaning which flows logically through history and allows persons to use their freedom in an inauthentic existence or in the dignity and greatness of creating with God a human future of powerful and positive possibilities. Partnership with God is mandatory, since God knows how to carve even the rotten wood and to ride the lame horse.

The church must help engage society in reflection and evaluation on the purpose of history and the responsibility persons play as cocreators with God in building the world of tomorrow. This action of the church involves the constructive criticisms of the social and political structures of society and the good news announcements of human possibilities and potentialities for justice and reconciliation.

The church can be effective as the leaven and light of the world. The church can assist the world in future building through the evangelistic ministry of proclamation and the servant ministry of a Christian presence in the marketplaces of education and economics as well as at the gates of government where secular elders make life and death shaping decisions.

The church as the custodian of good news announces a message of love in a world of alienation which frees persons from hostility and guilt as found in the law to a society of love based on the principles of God's grace and human forgiveness. This does not mean that society can see the church as an ecclesiastical utopia. It does mean that the church is the preacher of a Gospel which enables persons to live not in fear of catastrophe or war but with an openness to a coming new humanity, where the secular wastelands of today will become the human community of love.

Human Rights, Freedom, and Justice in the U.S.A.: A Black Perspective

Presented to the Commission on Freedom,
Justice, and Peace of the Baptist World
Alliance at Toronto, 1980.

Richard Wright was accurate in writing: "The history of the Negro in America is the history of America written in vivid and bloody terms. It is the history of men who tried to adjust themselves to a world whose laws, customs, and instruments of force were leveled against them. The Negro is America's metaphor."[1] The bloody history of black Americans in America at the hands of other nonviolent Americans, and the self-destructive behavior of blacks against blacks, plus the lives black Americans gave up on foreign battlefields as American soldiers, uniquely acquaint the race with the ugliness of Calvary and the cruelty of crucifixion.

The mournful tonal quality in Negro spirituals is not accidental. Sweat, pain, tears, and unmeasured agony caused by a multiplicity of crucifixions of innocent, helpless blacks gave authenticity to the query: "Were you there when they crucified my Lord?" The existential exposure to suffering provides the basis and explanation of the black Baptist fixation with the suffering servant who, prior to His ugly crucifixion, was a person of sorrows and acquainted with grief. The cross fixation revealed in black Baptist liturgy and proclamation is not the result of academic research and reflection, but the result of living for generations with human wrongs, oppression, and injustice.

Years before Martin Luther King, Jr., the Baptist apostle of freedom and nonviolence, uttered the clarion call which a rustic prophet named Amos uttered from Bethel, a forceful human rights leader called Marcus Garvey preached a gospel that was despised and rejected. In a speech given March 16, 1924, at Madison Square Garden, New York City, New York, Garvey said:

> We believe in justice and human love. If our rights are to be respected, then we too must respect the rights of all mankind; hence, we are ever ready and willing to yield to the white man the things that are his, and we feel that he, too, when his conscience is touched, will yield to us the things that are ours.[2]

In spite of centuries of denial, black Christian leadership has been positive and patient, urging the masses to work creatively and constructively in a nonsuicidal way for the realization of human rights, freedom, and justice. Black Christians and other persons of good will give their presences and purses to promote the nonviolent activity of King in the movement for human rights. They braved cattle prods, police dogs, fire hoses, angry mobs, and even the threat of death to pursue their quest for freedom and justice.

When eight prominent clergy persons sought to challenge King's methodology for attaining human rights in so-called Christian America, he responded by words from a Birmingham jail which are as powerful today as they were when they were written in 1963:

> But more basically, I am in Birmingham because injustice is here. Just as the prophets of the eighth century B.C. left their villages and carried their "thus saith the Lord" far beyond the boundaries of their hometowns,

and just as the Apostle Paul left his village of Tarsus and carried the gospel of Jesus Christ to the far corners of the Greco-Roman world, so am I compelled to carry the gospel of freedom beyond my own hometown. Like Paul, I must constantly respond to the Macedonian call for aid.[3]

The Christian leadership of King opened the door of human rights for other minorities and poor whites. For example, many poor, white children are now doing better in school because of Headstart programs, which resulted from black parents demanding that compensatory programs in education be established to offset the harm done by segregated education. Many poor, white young persons, as well as other minorities, are able to attend college on federal grants as a result of the black liberation struggle for equal opportunity in education. Health clinics and legal aid for the poor and lower classes of all ethnic groups owe their existence to the pioneering and prophetic efforts of King and other courageous Christian clergy persons.

Nevertheless, the gains other minorities and poor whites have made due to black advocacy and protest have not guaranteed full equality of opportunity, freedom, justice, and basic human rights to black Americans. After King's assassination, the era of black power emerged, asking for economic and political power in the decision-making processes of American life. Enemies of black power defined it to mean rioting, lawlessness, and the burning of buildings. With the exception of a few universities allowing a token faculty to establish a black studies curriculum alongside Asian studies and status-quo Anglo studies, the black power movement was aborted.

The pendulum moved from integration to a newer and more sophisticated form of racism among the respectable middle class. This movement gave us the philosophy of benign neglect. In 1970, Daniel Patrick Moynihan wrote President Richard Nixon a memo which said: "The American Negro is making extraordinary progress and the race issue in general could benefit from a period of benign neglect. We may need a period in which Negro progress continues and racial rhetoric fades."[4]

Black progress did not continue. Many gains made in the decade of the sixties eroded in the seventies. The America Nazi Party grew, and the Ku Klux Klan became vocal and visible from coast to coast. With this visibility, white Christians remained mute. No strong prophetic voices have emerged to condemn the increase of white, racist groups in America. Large groups of Caucasian Baptists have become preoccupied with inhouse debates over issues of doctrinal purity, while the great ethical issues, which relate to human survival and reconciliation, are dealt with by persons who have largely a humanistic and naturalistic orientation.

President William Augustus Jones of the Progressive National Baptist Convention has shared with me more than once his lament of the prophetic silence of white Baptists on the issues of race, Third-World oppression, and national and global injustice. Now a few black leaders share Jones' position. Among the respected leaders who are in agreement is Julian Bond, Georgia State Senator. At an N.A.A.C.P. fundraising dinner in San Francisco, November 28, 1979, Legislator Bond said:

> Blacks in the 1970s were America's forgotten people . . . the 70s was a decade of hiatus in the civil rights movement, a sleepy decade in which the thrust of the 60s was lost. It's almost like running in place and that amounts to a loss. The only reference to black people in *Newsweek's* wrapup on the 70s was to Muhammad Ali.[5]

In spite of a few vocal, elected officials such as Julian Bond, Ron Dellums, Shirley Chisholm, and mayors like Lionel Wilson of Oakland, California, Thomas Bradley of Los Angeles, California, and Richard Hatcher of Gary, Indiana, African Americans are underrepresented in the political process of America. Michael Goldstein, director of research for the Joint Center for Political Studies in Washington, D.C., says there are now only 4,607 black elected officials in the nation. This includes the District of Columbia and the Virgin Islands. That number is less than 1 percent of the 490,000 elected officials in the United States and only a 2 percent gain over last year.[6]

The tragedy of these figures is that too many young blacks are not taking advantage of their opportunities to vote because they have lost faith in the political process. They have forgotten how blood was shed in order to secure voting rights. Their historical memory is short, or they suffer from historical amnesia. Goldstein suggests other reasons for this apathy:

a. Electoral rules still discriminate against blacks, forcing them to gain voters by running at large rather than at district levels;
b. The black population tends to be a disadvantaged population, making it difficult for candidates to accumulate resources to run a campaign;
c. Many white voters are still reluctant to vote for black candidates;
d. Alienation among whites and blacks is increasing, especially among younger people of both races.[7]

This limited exposure to blacks gives the impression that blacks are inferior intellectually and morally and are possessors of a subexcellent culture. Hence, blackness symbolizes evil or badness, while whiteness symbolizes goodness or purity. Schoolchildren are taught to admire the speech of Patrick Henry in 1755, and never learn about the highly ethical David Walker's Appeal of 1829. In college and seminary, students read the scholarly works of Oscar Cullman, Karl Barth, and Emil Brunner without ever being exposed to the scholarly writings of black theologians like James Cone, J. DeOtis Roberts, and Henry H. Mitchell.

As far as black thinkers and proclaimers of the good news are concerned, the Caucasian validation of the black American experience as a source for relating the Christian faith to life comes from scholarly statements by very different scholars.

Olin P. Moyd argues: "The theology arising out of black religion has an abiding propensity toward existentialism."[8] Moyd acknowledges the concern of Nels Ferre that in the development of a Christology "one should not start with human experience because human limitations and self-centeredness may distort the truth which one perceives. Thus, what one discerns as truth may not be truth at all."[9] My response to Ferre is that if I look at my historical experience, both subjectively and objectively in the light of the living and resurrected Christ, who became man, suffered, bled, and died as I must do, then my Christological existentialism has veracity and integrity for me in my relationship to myself, to others, to nature, and to God the Creator, Sustainer, and Completer of human history.

Secondly, my friend at the American Baptist Seminary of the West, Bernard Ramm, defines cogently the existential approach in writing:

> The fundamental thesis of existentialism is that existence is prior to essence. This thesis means that my personal existence, my problem of being, my concern with my selfhood, my situation in the world is prior to and more fundamental than any theory about the world or reality. Man cannot begin with a theory of reality, a metaphysics or ontology: He can begin only where he is as a human being in the midst of all the contingencies of human existence. To attempt to begin anywhere else is to attempt the fantastic.[10]

We African Americans can only respond to the initiating act of God's love to us in Christ. We cannot help but visualize the Lord Jesus Christ in the Christological dimension of the liberation that he offers in our specific, concrete, historical, situation of living.

This is why James Cone, Professor of Theology, Union Theological Seminary, in New York City, wrote:

> There is no truth for and about black people that does not

emerge out of the context of their experience. Truth in that sense is black truth, a truth disclosed in the history and culture of black people. This means that there can be no Black Theology which does not take the black experience as a source for its starting point.[11]

Scholars who emphasize the transcendental aspect of God's nature and who emphasize the doctrine of revelation as a priority higher on the agenda of theology than the doctrine of creation or the doctrine of incarnation are deeply disturbed by the contextual and situational nature of black theology. Realizing the impossibility of defining God who transcends the limitations of language and human ability to organize sense from the sensory experiences of finite existence, it is still necessary to use human definitions of God in the light of human rights, freedom, and justice.

Western thinkers would do well to relate to the concerns of their Third World brothers and sisters in the household of Christian scholarship. In so doing, Asia speaks in saying: Theology is a living experience. It means "having rice with Jesus."[12] Latin America says: "Faith (or theology) is 'the action of love' within history."[13]

In 1966, while serving as a staff member of the Missionaries and Ministers Benefit Board of the American Baptist Churches, U.S.A., Dean R. Wright and William T. McKee allowed me to work with the Commission on Theological Perspectives of the National Committee on Black Churchmen in the U.S.A. As a participant on that committee, I helped write the following definition of black theology at the Interdenominational Theological Center in Atlanta, Georgia:

Black theology is a theology of black liberation. It seeks to plumb the black condition in the light of God's revelation in Jesus Christ, so that the black community can see that the gospel is commensurate with the achievement of black humanity. Black theology is a theology of "blackness." It is the affirmation of black humanity that emancipates black people from white racism, thus providing authentic freedom for both white and black people. It affirms the humanity of white people in that it says "no" to the encroachment of white oppression.[14]

In other words, the black church is a poor people's church. Those who belong to the black church are not the power-brokers, decision-makers, and the policy-shapers of the society. They are not the holders of great wealth or the heads of the academic, political, and ecclesiastical institutions of American society.

The words of the Apostle Paul to the Christians at Corinth apply to black Baptist Christians in relationship to human rights, freedom, and justice:

> Simply consider your own call . . . not many of you were wise, humanly speaking, not many mighty, not many noble, but God hath chosen the world's foolish things to put to shame the learned and God has chosen the weak in the world to shame the strong. God also has chosen the world's insignificant and despised people and nobodies in order to bring to nothing those who amount to something, so that nobody may boast in the presence of God (I Cor. 1: 26-29).

This Biblical source helps us understand why across the United States brave black Baptist pastors, with the full support of their congregations, proclaim that poverty is ugly, oppression is impermissible, and hunger in our technological society is unnecessary. Sin is not only metaphysically true but structurally suicidal in its personal and private dimensions and disastrous and destructive in its communal and collective manifestations.

Soteriology, or the doctrine of salvation, offers a remedy for sin as defined in the fall and for our sins which manifest the state of our sin. The doctrine of soteriology is predicated upon a sound Christology. Insight in this regard has been eloquently stated by Leonardo Boff:

A Christology that proclaims Jesus Christ as the Liberator seeks to be committed to the economic, social, and political liberation of those groups that are oppressed and dominated. It purports to see the theological relevance of the historic liberation of the vast majority of people on our continent. Such a Christology believes that its thinking and practice should be centered on such liberation. It seeks to create a style, and to develop the content of Christology in such a way that it can bring out the liberative dimensions present in Jesus' historical course.[15]

The style of the Allen Temple Baptist Church, of which I am pastor in Oakland, California, is spiritually oriented toward a warmhearted, passionate presentation of Jesus as the living Word and world Saviour who is to come again to usher in God's kingdom in its fullness. He has called us, His people, to a lifestyle of worship, proclamation, sacrifice, service, suffering, reconciling, and liberating action in love. We are not ashamed to announce that "God was in Christ, reconciling the world unto Himself, not imputing their trespasses unto them, and hath committed unto us the word of reconciliation" (II Cor. 5:19).

The Allen Temple Baptist Church has sought practical ways to join the activity of God in human rights. During 1979, the church led all of the churches of Oakland in securing memberships for the National Association for the Advancement of Colored People.

Members of the Christian Social Concerns Committee work tirelessly to monitor the meetings of the Oakland City Council, the Alameda County Board of Supervisors, and all governmental funding agencies that provide human services for the poor of all races. The pastor assists the Christian Social Concerns Committee in its prophetic role as an advocate for social justice through use of newspapers, television, and radio. Preaching applies, "Thus saith the Lord," to the current situations of challenge and crisis.

Voter registration campaigns and candidates' nights where

church members can question candidates about their ethical and moral values are also sponsored and supervised by the Committee on Christian Social Concerns.

Women's rights are very much the concern of the church family. There are battered wives and battered children in America society. Rape, incest, and brutality toward elderly parents all reveal the sickness of soul within American culture. In addition to providing counseling services and assisting the abused to find care in shelters and halfway houses, the Evangelism Committee works seriously in presenting to individuals, families, and even groups of persons who live more on street corners than in homes, the claims and promises of the Gospel.

Since the criminal justice system in America has such a poor reputation in meting our justice with an even hand, the Allen Temple men work very diligently to deter boys and young men from a lifestyle of crime. The extremely high black youth unemployment rate is a major contributing factor for the large number of black youths who are not held in detention halls, juvenile halls, jails, and prisons. The Allen Temple Job Information Center led a group of professionals in the church in sponsoring a job fair and career day to help unemployed persons secure employment and to give vocational guidance to young persons.

Many inner city blacks reside in highrise housing projects or in housing tracts that have extremely high incidences of crime. In cities where minorities and the poor cannot afford decent housing with fair rents, great harm is done to human dignity. The Allen Temple Baptist Church, in cooperation with the United East Oakland Clergy, is working with local housing groups to solve these problems.

The church of Jesus Christ, in order to promote freedom, justice, and human rights, must look again at her own reservations about allowing women freely and fully to use the talents of their God-given potential in service for Jesus Christ. Outstanding women in ministry at Allen Temple have provided a needed dynamic in various leadership positions.

Demographers report that Hispanics are the fastest-growing minority group in the United States and are expected to overtake blacks as the nation's largest minority before 1985. The Hispanic population is young and urban. In sharing with them our freedom in Jesus Christ, we must be able to talk to them in their native tongue. A class in conversational Spanish is preparing persons to minister in Christ's love to the Hispanic community.

Conclusion

In the quest for human rights, freedom, and justice, the black church must remain true to the Gospel of Jesus Christ. Because of Jesus, we learn that we can live in peace with our God, with ourselves, and with our fellow human beings. Our experiences as Christian black "persons" have taught us to identify with people who hurt around the world. Our prayer is that of Martin Luther King, Jr., "that the dark clouds of racial prejudice will soon pass away, and the deep fog of misunderstanding will be lifted from our fear-drenched communities, and in some not too distant tomorrow the radiant stars of love . . . will shine over our great nation with all their scintilating beauty."[16]

Pious passivity will not make this dream a reality. Baptists in America, in cooperation with other Christian brothers and sisters, can purge racism from the dimensions of denominational structures, especially where church investments support apartheid in South Africa, and where mission boards support triage as a strategy for meeting the hunger needs of the Third World. The debate on nineteenth-century theological questions, no longer asked by the modern world, ignores the cries of the oppressed in the barrios, ghettos, prisons, unemployment lines, and street corners of American inner cities. Verbalizing the faith with words of confession and commitment is not enough. We must not become the religious legalists of our own day. "This people draweth nigh unto me with their mouth, and honoreth me with their lips, but their heart is far from me" (Matt. 15:8).

God is waiting on us and expects us to be his coworkers.

God is not only with us, in us, and for us but God also is judg-
ing us in Christ. He invites us to adopt lifestyles which affirm
the partial presence of the rule of God and which will be
faithful in witness and service until Jesus, the Lord of liberation comes again to usher in the fullness of the kingdom of
God.

FOOTNOTES:

¹Edited by William M. Chace and Peter Collier, *Justice Denied: The Black Man in America* (New York, Chicago, San Francisco, Atlanta: Harcourt, Brace and World, 1970), p. V.

²Ibid., p. 247.

³Ibid., p. 341.

⁴Oakland *Tribune*, Sunday, December 23, 1979, Section D, p. 4.

⁵Ibid., p. 4.

⁶Ibid., p. 4.

⁷Ibid., p. 4.

⁸Olin P. Moyd, *Redemption in Black Theology* (Valley Forge, Pennsylvania: Judson Press, 1979), p. 93.

⁹Ibid., p. 93.

¹⁰Ibid., p. 93.

¹¹James Cone, *God of the Oppressed* (New York: Seabury Press, 1975), p. 17.

¹²Allan Aubrey Boesak: *Farewell to Innocence* (Maryknoll, New York: Orbis Books, 1976), p. 17.

¹³Ibid., p. 12.

¹⁴Ibid., p. 11.

¹⁵Leonardo Boff, *Jesus Christ Liberator: A Critical Christology for Our Time.* Translated from Spanish by Patrick Hughes (Maryknoll, New York: Orbis Books, 1978), p. 266.

¹⁶Martin Luther King, Jr., *Why We Can't Wait* (New York and Toronto: A Signet Book, published by The New American Library, 1963, 1964), p. 95.